TalkAbility

*People skills for verbal children
on the autism spectrum – A guide for parents*

FERN SUSSMAN

The
Hanen
Program®

A Hanen Centre Publication

TalkAbility™
By Fern Sussman

The
Hanen
Program.

A Hanen Centre Publication

The Hanen Program, The Parent-Child Logo and TalkAbility are trademarks owned
by Hanen Early Language Program

Library and Archives Canada Cataloging in Publication

Sussman, Fern, 2006
TalkAbility: People Skills for Verbal Children on the Autism Spectrum –
A Guide for Parents/ Fern Sussman.

ISBN 0-921145-32-2

1. Language acquisition – Parent participation. 2. Children – Language.
3. Interpersonal communication between children. 4. Asperger Syndrome.
5. Autism

I. Sussman, Fern   II. Hanen Centre

Copies of this book may be ordered from the publisher:

The Hanen Centre
1075 Bay Street, Suite 515
Toronto, ON
Canada M5S 2B1

Telephone: (416) 921-1073
Fax: (416) 921-1225
Email: info@hanen.org
Web: www.hanen.org

Parts of this book were adapted from *More Than Words: Helping Parents
Promote Communication and Social Skills in Children with Autism Spectrum Disorder*
by Fern Sussman (1999) and *Learning Language and Loving It:
A Guide to Promoting Children's Social, Language, and Literacy Development in Early
Childhood Settings* by Elaine Weitzman and Janice Greenberg (2002),
both Hanen Centre publications.

Illustrations: Kitty Macaulay
Design: Disruptor/ Kevin Connolly
Editor: Making Words Work/ Martin Townsend

Printed in Canada by Transcontinental Interglobe Inc.

Contents

Acknowledgements

I am indebted to the many people who made this book possible. To begin with, I had the good fortune to have the support of Elaine Weitzman, Executive Director of The Hanen Centre. I can't thank her enough for her time, her intellect, her support and her keen sense of what is readable. I appreciate her help in keeping me on track every step of the way.

This book started as a collaboration with Cheri Rorabeck, one of the brightest and most dedicated speech-language pathologists I know. Cheri tirelessly sat at my kitchen table for hundreds of hours to help create the parent training program on which this book is based.

Over the years, I have had the opportunity to work with an amazing group of colleagues who have always been willing to share their insights into how children interact and how language develops. A special thanks to Janice Greenberg, Program Manager for the Learning Language and Loving It Program, who has the office next to mine; Janice always bolstered my spirit and made me feel that this book was worthwhile.

Thanks to the other talented Hanen Program Managers: Cindy Conklin, Cindy Earle, Michelle Lintott and Barb Wylde. And a special thanks to Penny Tantakis, The Hanen Centre's Marketing and Operations Manager and so much more. On Penny's team is Angie Velarde, our Sales Coordinator, someone who cares deeply about giving parents the tools they need to help their children develop to their fullest potential. I'd also like to acknowledge the efforts of the entire Hanen Centre staff: Teresinha Costa, Sara Coutinho, Jennifer Cunningham, Dani Cooperman, Joanna Horobin, Tom Khan, Lorie Kientz, Edilberto Navas, Lawrence Rose, Teresa Sartori, Les Turner and Sandy Wong.

A team of speech-language pathologists who are experts in the field of autism read the first drafts of *TalkAbility* and gave me invaluable feedback. Many thanks to Ian Roth, Cheri Rorabeck, Lauren Lowry and Sue Honeyman.

The ideas in this book come alive in Kitty Macaulay's beautiful drawings. Each picture shines with her care and tenderness. Not only is Kitty extremely talented, but she remained calm during computer breakdowns and a personal loss. Martin Townsend, editor supreme, performed magic with my words, making me sound better and offering suggestions that went way beyond his role as editor. And Kevin Connolly at Disruptor contributed his beautiful design, patience, creativity and willingness to think outside the box.

Research shows that parents are the best teachers of their own children. I didn't need any randomized trial to reach that conclusion. Every time I have visited families in their homes, I've been privileged to see first-hand the powerful effect a loving and nurturing parent can have on a child. I am forever grateful to the parents in this program's pilot groups, from whom I learned so much.

Finally, thanks to my husband, Jackie, for always listening, for naming this book and for giving me his unconditional love and support. Thanks to my wonderful grown-up children, Jillian and Matthew, who have shown me that, as a parent, I must have done a couple of things right. Thanks to my good friend Adele Ostfield for always expressing an interest in what I was doing, and to my mother-in-law, Frances Sussman, for a weekly supply of baked goods. And thanks to my own parents, Lillian and Maurice Goodman, whom I am lucky to still have in my life as mentors.

Get Started Here

Some people seem to know what to do and say in every situation. They can always strike up a conversation and keep it going. These "sociable" people are easy to talk to and fun to be around.

Many sociable adults were sociable as children, too. They were the ones who had lots of friends. They fit in easily at school and on the playground.

But not every child feels comfortable in social situations. Many children have a hard time playing and talking with other children, and they don't know how to go about making friends.

Who This Book Is For

This book is for parents and caregivers of young children who have difficulty interacting with others. To find out if this book can help you and your child, consider the following questions:

> Does your child find having a conversation hard?
> Does your child shy away from other children?
> Does your child insist on talking to other children about things they have no interest in?
> Does your child want to play only with certain toys and refuse to try new things?
> Does your child become upset if his or her routines change?

If you answered "yes" to any one of these questions, this book can help you.

The ideas in this book are useful for children between the ages of 3 and 7. Some of these children may have a diagnosis of Asperger Syndrome (AS), High-Functioning Autism (HFA) or Nonverbal Learning Disorder (NLD). Others may have no diagnosis at all. Most of these young children can talk well and seem bright. All of them, however, have difficulty knowing what to do and say in social situations.

What This Book Is About

TalkAbility offers a simple approach to helping your child develop better social skills, so he or she can have conversations and make friends more easily. This book will also help you find the best ways to interact with your child. *TalkAbility* isn't about teaching skills through drills or memorization. It's about giving your child new opportunities to learn by doing—by socializing with you in everyday situations.

This book is divided into two parts:

Chapters 1–9: You and Your Child
The first part of the book focuses on your child's first meaningful conversations—the ones he or she has with you. You'll learn how to help your child take a turn in a conversation and then wait for you to take yours. You'll find out how to help your child understand the meaning behind the words—all the subtle messages you send with facial expressions and body language. You'll also find information on how to help your child tell stories and play imaginatively.

Chapters 10–13: You, Your Child and Your Child's First Friends
The last part of the book focuses on how you can help your child make friends. You'll learn how to support your child so that he or she can play successfully with other children and enjoy making friends.

What Results You Can Expect

Beginning with the first chapter, you can expect to learn some easy ways to help your child in social situations. As you start using the suggestions in this book, you may find a change in your relationship with your child. Your conversations with him or her will probably be less one-sided; they'll begin to sound more like a back-and-forth sharing of ideas. With a little coaching from you, your child will start to find out that playing with others can be fun once you know how to go about it.

As the two of you begin putting *TalkAbility*'s ideas into practice, however, keep in mind that children have different personalities and different ways of learning. And remember that, even when your child becomes more sociable, there will still be times when he or she will want to be alone—and that's okay!

1

How Your Child Learns

No two children learn exactly the same way. Knowing how your child learns best will help you make it easier for him to learn. Chapter 1 of *TalkAbility* will help you understand your child's natural learning style.

This first chapter will also help you examine how your child is affected by the way you talk with him and act when you're around him. You'll see that adjusting these things can produce powerful results.

Understand Your Child's Learning Style

Knowing how your child learns best will answer a lot of questions about the kind of support he needs from you now. His natural learning style—the way he approaches the world—makes sense to him, but it may also present barriers to successful socializing.

For a better understanding of your child's individual learning style, take a moment to consider these questions: Does your child learn best by talking about things, or by looking at pictures or printed words? Does he memorize facts, or even whole chunks of what he hears? Does he focus on details or look at "the big picture"? Does he try out new things or stick to what he's familiar with?

Read on to find out what kind of learning style your child has and what this means.

Is your child a verbal or visual learner?

Some children have good verbal skills. They can learn a lot about social situations by talking about them with you. Other children are visual learners. They understand what they see better than what they hear. Adding "visual cues" such as pictures and written words to your explanations can greatly help these children make sense of what's going on. Of course, to some extent, most children learn both verbally and visually.

Check the boxes below to find out whether your child is a verbal learner, a visual learner or a combination of the two. This book will give you ideas for ways to help both kinds of learners.

Visual learner

My child:

- ☑ Likes puzzles
- ○ Likes to draw pictures
- ○ Enjoys building with blocks or Lego
- ☑ Remembers what he sees (for example, he knows the exact route to Grandma's house)
- ○ Likes to watch game shows on TV that use letters
- ☑ Likes books
- ○ Can read some words

This is our new TV. It's got a DVD player built right in the front.

Jackson can get confused by his mom's descriptions. Looking at a picture helps him understand what she is talking about.

Verbal learner

My child:

○ Speaks like an adult

☑ Has a good vocabulary

☑ Likes to list the things he's interested in (such as the names of countries, dinosaurs or action heroes)

○ Likes to talk about what's going on now or what happened in the past

☑ Sometimes uses memorized phrases or sentences

○ Often initiates conversations

○ Likes conversations that he initiates

Ali learns by talking and listening.

Basically, visual learners learn best by looking; verbal learners learn by talking and listening. As important as this distinction is, it's just one way of looking at different learning styles. Several more ways are described on the following pages.

> **Clues to Knowing Your Child's Learning Style**
>
> No one likes labelling a child. But a diagnosis may give you insight into your child's behaviour—including information about his learning style. Because children with Asperger Syndrome (AS) and Nonverbal Learning Disorder (NLD) usually talk well, they learn best through discussion. Of course, seeing social situations explained in stories and pictures may also help them understand. These kinds of visual helpers are especially effective with strong visual learners, including many children with High-Functioning Autism (HFA).

What kind of memory does your child have?

Learning by memorizing

Many children with HFA or AS acquire information by memorizing lots of facts. When they are young, these children focus on information that they can learn in the form of lists, such as numbers and letters. When they are older, they memorize many facts about a specific topic.

If your child is this kind of learner, he might sound very smart and impressive. But he can also be inflexible about what he wants to talk about and do.

Learning in chunks

Using "echolalia"—repeating words and sentences produced by others—is the way all children learn to say new things. Most children stop parroting others as soon as they can find their own original ways of saying things. Perhaps your child still uses a chunk lifted from a video, a song or even another situation when he can't think of his own words. Using someone else's words is the best way he can express himself at the time.

As your child starts to understand that each word has a specific meaning, his own spontaneous speech will replace the echolalia. There could also be a few phrases that your child repeats that don't seem to serve any purpose besides calming him down in stressful situations. When he has another, equally effective way to make himself feel better, he'll stop doing that, too.

Children who learn in chunks can also miss the meaning of what people say because they can't break the whole sentence down into its parts. For example, your child might be used to hearing you say, "Give me five!" But if you change what you say to "Give me five kisses," he might still expect you to high-five him. He makes this mistake because he associates any sentence that starts with "give me five" with a certain action.

Losing the game isn't really the worst thing to happen to Ali. He's just expressing his feelings by repeating word-for-word something he's heard a character in a video say.

Does your child like to try new things?

There is a part of the human brain that is excited by new things just because they're new. But in some people, this part of the brain doesn't work that way. If your child doesn't notice new things or is actually afraid of trying anything different, it's probably because his brain works differently.

If you know that your child likes things to stay the same, help him prepare for changes by giving him lots of warning before they happen. Also, try not to introduce too many changes at one time.

Does your child worry?

Besides changes in their routines, there are many other things that some children worry about. Being overly anxious can keep your child from joining in activities. If you can identify what bothers him, you'll be able to help him when he's feeling anxious and even before his anxiety starts. Check the boxes that describe your child.

- ○ My child is afraid of the dark.
- ○ My child is afraid of dogs or insects.
- ○ My child has to do some things over and over again.
- ○ My child worries about being away from me.
- ○ My child worries that something bad will happen.
- ○ My child gets anxious before school or a play date.
- ○ My child worries in other ways.

Once you know what bothers your child, you can help him prepare for a stressful situation before it arises. Sometimes, all you need to do is change the environment. That might mean leaving a night light on if your child is afraid of the dark or covering up a picture in the house that upsets him. Different children respond well to different calming methods. Many children relax when they do something physical. Another way to help your child feel calmer is to get him used to what bothers him by exposing him to it gradually. If he's afraid of the dark, for instance, start by playing games in a darkened room, like finding hidden treats with a flashlight.

Children with anxieties need to learn ways to calm themselves down when they're feeling anxious. For example, if your child is afraid of dogs, he might sing songs to distract himself when he passes by one. Your child can learn how to relax himself by taking a few, slow deep breaths (breathing in through his nose and out through his mouth).

Is your child interested in the big picture or details?

When most of us look at something, we see "the big picture"—we understand it as a whole. We don't see each and every detail.

For example, as soon as we see a piece of writing paper, we know that it's used for writing. Usually, we don't think about its other features (it's white, flat, square and has lines on it). But many children with AS or HFA focus on these kinds of details first. They use the parts (not the whole) to make sense of the world.

It's hard for these children to understand that there is more than one way to figure out what something is. Imagine seeing an old woman walking with a cane—and then deciding that all old people use canes.

Think about whether your child focuses on the details. If he does, you're going to have to give him extra help to see the big picture.

Understand Your Child's Sensory Needs

We take in information about the world through our senses: sight, hearing, taste, smell and touch. Besides the five senses, our perception of the world around us is also affected by our sense of movement and sense of balance. Ordinarily, we don't have to think about all the information our senses collect. Our brain does the sorting work for us, blocking out certain sensations so we can pay attention to more important ones.

Your child might sense things in a slightly different way from you or me. He may sometimes experience "sensory overload," or he may be over-sensitive or under-sensitive to certain things. To learn (and to talk and play) to the best of his ability, he may need your help to deal with these difficulties first.

Does your child experience sensory overload?

Sometimes children's brains can't sort out all of the sensations coming in at once. This experience is known as "sensory overload."

Not surprisingly, sensory overload can lead children to shut other people out. It's hard to be sociable if you're constantly distracted by sounds or lights.

When he's at home, Matthew has no problem talking to his sister about his favourite race cars.

Alana, that's a Radical VR8. This one's a Radical SR3. It's the fastest race car.

You have the Rad VR8.

At school, Matthew looks like a different child. Overwhelmed by the noise in the classroom, he can't join in a conversation on his favourite topic.

Is your child over-sensitive to some things?

Some children are over-sensitive to certain sensations. In other words, it takes only a small amount of the sensation to make them feel uncomfortable.

If your child is over-sensitive, he may try to avoid the sensations that bother him. He may look anxious or fearful. For example, he might cover his ears when he hears the vacuum cleaner. Or, like Emily in the picture below, he might cope with what's bothering him by running out of the room.

Emily is over-sensitive to noise. She finds Aunt Rhoda's voice too loud, so she runs away.

WHERE'S MY EMILY?

Jake is over-sensitive to movement. He lies down so he can feel the ground with his whole body and stay still.

Jake, sit up so you can see the picture.

Is your child under-sensitive to some things?

Maybe your child is under-sensitive to certain sensations. That means it takes a lot of a stimulation to make him react—for instance, a very bright light or a very loud noise.

Sometimes an under-sensitive child may not look interested in what's happening. He might have difficulty paying attention to you. When he gets a lot of stimulation, he feels energized and better able to cope. So he seeks these sensations out to feel "just right"—as Ethan does on the next page.

Ethan is under-sensitive to movement. He needs to run before he's ready to sit.

Ethan's mother thinks he doesn't feel like being sociable. But Ethan isn't really avoiding Sarah. To feel comfortable, he needs to stimulate his sense of movement by running. He gets the same good feeling from climbing, jumping and going very high on swings and seesaws.

It's possible that your child is both over-sensitive to some sensations and under-sensitive to others. For example, he might not respond when you call his name (under-sensitive to speech) but cover his ears when he hears a dog barking (over-sensitive to certain sounds).

Help your child cope with his sensitivities

Emily's, Jake's and Ethan's actions show us how they deal with their sensitivities. When their parents understand their special sensory needs, they can give them better ways of coping.

For example, Emily's mother could ask Aunt Rhoda to speak softly. Even better, she could encourage Emily to ask politely herself. Jake's mother could find Jake a chair to sit on so he can sit straight with his feet firmly on the ground, giving him the stability that he needs. Ethan's mother might consider a game of chase before lunch. That way, Ethan can get the movement he needs before having to sit.

You may have to show your child how to handle a variety of different sensations so he's ready to be sociable. Later, your child might use your suggestions to keep himself calm and alert.

If Ethan has a chance to run first, he'll be ready to sit at the table.

To learn more about your child's sensory preferences, fill in the Sensory Checklist on the next three pages. Once you can identify what kinds of sensations he likes and dislikes, you'll have taken a big step toward making sure your child is in the right frame of mind to be sociable. If you need more guidance on this topic, an occupational therapist might be able to help.

Sensory Checklist

Movement/Balance

My child is under-sensitive to movement. He shows the need for movement by...

- ☑ Running/rocking/spinning
- ☑ Climbing on counters
- ○ Wriggling in his seat
- ○ Other: _____

Some suggestions:
- Try running games, like tag or races.
- Give your child a lot of opportunity to play on playground equipment such as swings, slides and seesaws.

My child is over-sensitive to movement. He shows that movement makes him uncomfortable by...

- ○ Getting upset on escalators, swings, see-saws or slides
- ○ Lying on the floor
- ○ Expressing a dislike of movement games (such as baseball, basketball or somersaults)
- ○ Other: _____

Some suggestions:
- Try to help your child learn table top games, such as board games and other activities during which he can sit still.
- Make sure your child's feet can touch the ground when he sits.

Touch

My child is under-sensitive to touch and shows his need for it. He...

- ○ Wants big hugs
- ○ Insists on wearing tight-fitting clothes
- ○ Likes crunchy, chewy foods
- ○ Leans on other people
- ○ Chews on his clothing
- ○ Likes climbing on furniture and people
- ○ Other: _____

Some suggestions:

- Give your child firm handshakes or high-fives during the day.
- Read touch-and-feel books. For example, find or make an animal book with something like a duck covered in feathers or a sheep made out of soft yarn.
- Let your child guess what objects are by touching them only.
- Play clapping games, such as pat-a-cake or taking turns putting hands on top of the other person's.
- Let your child punch a punching bag a few times a day.
- Keep hand toys—such as squishy balls, little cars or figures—ready for your child.

My child shows he is over-sensitive to touch. He . . .

- ○ Dislikes certain clothing textures
- ○ Dislikes wearing hats and gloves
- ○ Dislikes getting his hair washed or cut
- ○ Dislikes sitting or standing close to others
- ○ Doesn't want to finger-paint or use playdough
- ○ Other: _____

Some suggestions:

- Find loose clothes and let your child wear mittens instead of gloves.
- Let your child paint with a brush, or manipulate the playdough with a spatula if he doesn't want to touch it.

Hearing

My child is under-sensitive to sound. He . . .

- ○ Doesn't always respond to his name
- ○ Doesn't appear to hear what people say
- ○ Likes certain music and sounds
- ○ Tunes out in the middle of a conversation
- ○ Other: _____

Some suggestions:

- Put animation in your voice to help your child pay attention to what you say.
- Try singing to get your child's attention.

My child is over-sensitive to sound. He . . .

- ○ Gets upset in noisy rooms
- ○ Hears the faintest sound
- ○ Wants me to use a soft voice (especially when he's upset)
- ○ Doesn't want me to talk a lot (especially when he's upset)
- ○ Gets upset by loud noises
- ○ Covers his hears when he hears certain sounds
- ○ Other: _____

Sensory Checklist continued

Some suggestions:
- Talk softly and stay calm.
- Speak in short, simple sentences and don't say too much at one time.
- Have earplugs ready for noisy rooms.

Sight

My child is under-sensitive to things he sees. He ...

- ◯ Likes game shows with printed questions on the screen
- ◯ Likes lining things up
- ◯ Likes watching moving objects (such as revolving doors, fans)
- ◯ Likes to look at his toys while lying on the ground
- ◯ Other: _____

Some suggestions:
- Go on a hunt for hidden toys with a flashlight.
- Write notes to your child. Put them in his lunch bag or on his pillow.
- Watch videos together.

My child is over-sensitive to things he sees. He ...

- ◯ Turns the lights down low
- ◯ Doesn't like looking at the print in books
- ◯ Blocks his eyes from the sun
- ◯ Other: _____

Some suggestions:
- Have your child's sunglasses handy.
- Keep the lights dimmed.

> **Does your child have difficulty with motor planning?**
>
> In addition to sensory problems, many children with AS or HFA have "motor planning" problems. If your child has these kinds of problems, it will be hard for him to play some simple games, like catch or jump rope. He might have trouble holding a pencil. You can imagine how being unable to do things like these will affect his play with other children.
>
> *Your child might have motor planning problems if he does any of the following:*
> > Bumps into things and people
> > Looks clumsy
> > Plays with toys the same way over and over
> > Walks in an unusual way
> > Plays with something once and then leaves
>
> *Suggestions:*
> > Touch your child to physically remind him where he's going and what he's doing.
> > Make some visual cues. For example, if your child goes down a slide one time only, try making some footprints out of paper so he can follow them from the bottom of the slide back to the first step on the slide ladder.

Look at Your Interaction Style

Your interaction style—how you act and talk with your child—has an enormous effect on him. Remember Emily's loud-talking aunt? That's one example (a negative one) of how an adult's interaction style can affect the way a child talks or plays.

Take the following quiz to find out what your interaction style is. Answer "Yes" to the questions that describe how you act *most* of the time.

WHERE'S MY EMILY?

		Yes	No
1.	I ask my child a lot of questions.	○ Yes	○ No
2.	I often tell my child what to do or say.	○ Yes	○ No
3.	I decide what my child and I will play or talk about.	○ Yes	○ No
4.	I let my child choose the games we play.	○ Yes	○ No
5.	I talk about what my child wants to talk about.	○ Yes	○ No
6.	I speak softly when I talk to my child.	○ Yes	● No
7.	I speak loudly when I talk to my child.	○ Yes	○ No
8.	I am very animated when I talk to my child.	○ Yes	○ No
9.	I like to play quiet games, like board games, with my child.	○ Yes	○ No
10.	I like to play rough and tumble games with my child.	○ Yes	○ No

Calm style

If you said that...

> You speak softly to your child (#6)
> You like to play quiet games (#9)
> You don't speak loudly to your child (#7)
> You aren't very animated when you talk to your child (#8)
> You don't like to play rough and tumble games with your child (#10)

... you may have a calm style.

People with a calm style react to stressful situations without getting nervous or excited. They speak slowly and seldom raise their voices. They tend to have a soothing effect on those around them. A parent with a calm style is a good match for a child who is over-sensitive to his surroundings.

Exciting style

If you said that...

> You speak loudly to your child (#7)
> You are very animated when you talk to your child (#8)
> You like to play rough and tumble games with your child (#10)
> You don't speak softly to your child (#6)
> You don't like to play quiet games with your child (#9)

... you may have an "exciting" style.

Some of us try to make everything exciting for our child with our voices and actions. We use a loud voice with a lot of animation. People with an exciting style use big hand gestures and movement when they talk. Most of us consider them a lot of fun to be around. A parent with an exciting style is a good match for a child who is under-sensitive to any of the sensations, such as sound, touch or sight.

Match your style to your child's needs

Once you figure out whether your own style is calm or exciting, decide if it's the right match for your child. You can turn around situations simply by changing your style. You could also suggest that other people in your child's life—relatives, teachers, playmates—do the same.

Changing your style usually isn't as challenging as it sounds. If a calm style isn't your natural approach, you may have to learn how to create a calm atmosphere. For example, if your child covers his ears or gets upset during a loud discussion in a brightly lit room, try dimming the lights and using a quiet voice. Or, if your child is under-sensitive and doesn't pay attention when you talk to him, try using an animated voice and lots of hand gestures.

When Aunt Rhoda tones
down, Emily tunes in.

> A CALM STYLE is a good match for an OVER-SENSITIVE child.
> An EXCITING STYLE is a good match for an UNDER-SENSITIVE child.

Directive style   Oho noho!

If you said that...

> You ask your child a lot of questions (#1)
> You often tell your child what to do or say (#2)
> You decide what you and your child will play or talk about (#3)
> You don't let your child choose the games you play (#4)
> You don't talk about what your child wants to talk about (#5)

...you probably have a directive style.

When Luke's mother uses a directive
style, Luke doesn't say anything.

Parents who use a directive style with their child usually ask a lot of questions. They often tell their child (or show him) exactly what to do. Parents like this probably feel that their child needs a lot of help to succeed at learning new things.

Sometimes the directive approach does work. But parents with this style often ask too many questions and give too many directions. "Directors" often want their child to give them the "right" answer, so they ask a lot of questions until they get the response they're looking for.

But does the directive style help children learn? Yes and no—see the box below.

> **How a Child Reacts to a Directive Style**
>
> > He responds to questions and follows directions.
> > He learns new skills like how to play with a hard-to-operate toy or what to say to greet a friend. ☺
> > He waits for someone else to initiate play and conversation. ☹
> > He feels pressured to say or do something and may give up. ☹
> > He gives one-word responses. ☹
> > He repeats what you say instead of using his own words (echolalia). ☹

Responsive style

If you said that...

> You let your child choose the games you play (#4)
> You talk about what your child wants to talk about (#5)
> You don't ask your child a lot of questions (#1)
> You don't often tell your child what to do and say (#2)
> You don't decide what your child will play or talk about (#3)

... you may have a responsive style.

Luke says more when his mother follows his lead.

Parents with a responsive style wait and let their child take the lead in deciding what to play and talk about. Then, they respond to what the child has said—which makes the child want to take another turn in the conversation. This is sometimes called a "Follow Your Child's Lead" approach.

Children start more conversations on their own and talk more when their parents use a responsive style. So, most of the time you'll want to use this style: waiting to see what interests your child and then building on those interests. But being responsive doesn't mean never asking questions or telling your child what to do. If you ask the right questions at the right time, you can keep your child in the conversation. If you give clear directions, your child can learn a new skill.

How a Child Reacts to a Responsive Style

> He feels powerful. ☺

> He initiates more play and conversation on his own. ☺

> There are fewer arguments because he chooses what he wants to do. ☺

> He is more sociable. ☺

> He uses longer, more complex sentences. ☺

> He talks more about his own ideas. ☺

Knowing how your child learns and how your interaction style affects him will help you figure out what makes him feel relaxed, alert and ready to interact. Changing your style will likely be a trial-and-error process. What works one time might not work the next time, but it could be successful the time after that. At first, it's desirable to have a few different ideas to fall back on.

Whenever possible, ask your child what makes him feel the best. After all, as he gets older, he's going to have to tell others what helps him and find his own ways to keep himself focused on what's going on around him.

2

Help Your Child Understand What You Say Without Words

It's okay, Mom. I can have crackers!

Conversation consists of much more than just words. The messages contained in people's facial expressions and gestures are often just as important as what is actually said.

For most of us, "reading" these wordless messages comes as naturally as walking or eating. We can learn much about a person's thoughts just by keeping our eyes open during conversation. Our ears pick up similar messages, beyond the words, in the other person's voice.

Children who notice these unspoken messages usually talk and play with other children easily. They understand what their playmates want and feel just by looking at them. But if your child has trouble reading these clues, socializing will be much harder. In this chapter and throughout the rest of the book, you'll learn ways to help your child pick up what the people around him are saying without words.

What We Say Without Words

Your actions and facial expressions give your child strong clues about how you're feeling and what you're thinking. In the picture on the previous page, Jackson's mother never says that she is sad or disappointed. But Jackson "reads" the message on her face and in her body language, and he sees the empty cookie jar. As soon as he understands how his mother feels, he tries to make her feel better.

Think about all the ways we pick up wordless messages during conversation:

> Voice—how rapidly or slowly our conversation partners are talking, and how loudly or softly; where their pauses are; which words they stress
> Body language—how and where the other people are standing; what they're doing as they speak or listen; which gestures they make with their hands
> Facial expression—what feelings they show with their eyes, nose and mouth
> The situation—what's going on at the time; what happened before
> The person—who is sending the message (For example, "Stop!" might mean one thing when a police officer says it and another thing when your best friend does.)

A child who reads these messages well can do three important things. He can understand the meaning behind the words people say. He can often predict what people will do. And he can respond appropriately (for instance, he can change what he says if someone looks confused, or show empathy if someone looks sad). With your help, your child can develop stronger "people skills" that will make conversation easier and play more fun.

Face-reading

In most children, the ability to read wordless (or nonverbal) messages on other people's faces develops slowly in the first years of life. Chances are that, when your child was a baby, he didn't learn to pay attention to nonverbal communication, and especially to facial expressions. For example, he probably didn't notice the raised eyebrows and wide-open eyes that show surprise and fear.

If you look at how face-reading develops in most children, you'll have a better idea of the basic learning stages your child probably still needs to go through to improve his social skills. Most children begin face-reading in infancy as they search their parents' faces for signs of comfort. Later on, they learn to follow their mother's "eye gaze"—to look in the direction she's looking in. At first this may happen only when Mom turns her head in the same direction as she looks; then, as time goes on, the baby doesn't need that cue any more.

During their first year, babies continue to check their parents' faces for reactions. They want to know, "Am I doing okay?" As they watch their parents' reactions to the world around them, they figure out how they should feel about things. For example, the child may have learned that raised eyebrows and eyes open wide are signs of surprise or fear. So if he sees this look on his mother's face when a dog runs up, he'll probably decide he's also scared of dogs. If his mother smiles and reaches out to pet the dog, he'll likely want to touch the dog, too.

Between two and five years, children learn to identify other people's feelings by looking at their faces. Children recognize happiness first, followed by sadness or anger, and then surprise and fear.

As children grow up, they continue to look at the faces of the people they're talking with. Of course, most of us don't look at the other person every second we're having a conversation. We look more when we're listening than when we're talking. That's because by watching other people's faces, especially their eyes, we can find the meaning behind their words (as Christopher and Tyler do on the next page).

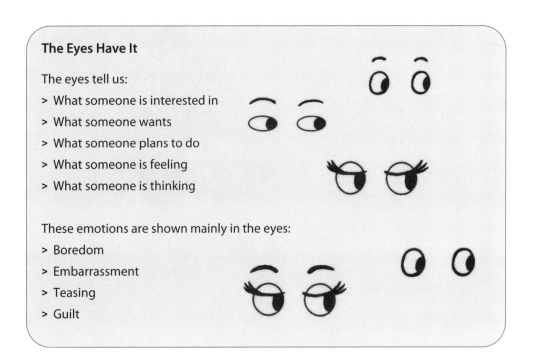

The Eyes Have It

The eyes tell us:

> What someone is interested in
> What someone wants
> What someone plans to do
> What someone is feeling
> What someone is thinking

These emotions are shown mainly in the eyes:

> Boredom
> Embarrassment
> Teasing
> Guilt

Christopher knows exactly what Mom is feeling and thinking from observing her face and body language.

Tyler can tell exactly what Dad wants by noticing what he's looking at.

You may recall that, when your child was a baby, he never paid much attention to your face. Perhaps you remember thinking that when he did look at your face, he focused on your mouth. And you're probably right. Children who have trouble socializing have often missed out on the early learning stage of paying attention to faces. When these children do look, they tend to look at one area of the face at a time, and it's usually the mouth.

Sometimes, an emotion is revealed in all parts of the face. So your child may be able to tell if you're happy, sad, angry, scared or surprised by looking only at your eyes and eyebrows, or only your nose and mouth. Your eyes, however, are where the most information lies. Only your eyes can help him figure out more complex feelings such as whether you're teasing or feeling unsure.

James, I wonder who else is going to be at Grandma's tonight.

Maybe Uncle Rob!

The look on Mom's face lets James see that she expects him to continue the conversation.

Look at the chart below. It shows you some of the ways people's faces can express their feelings.

Simple Feelings (The Whole Face Matters)

Feeling	What the Eye Area May Look Like	What the Mouth and Nose May Look Like
Happy	Eyes crinkled at the outer corners	Mouth corners turned upward in smile
Sad	Eyebrows lowered in a frown and forehead creased Eyes appear smaller Eyes look down Eyes filling with tears	Mouth corners turned downward Lips narrowed to a thin line Lower lip protrudes over upper lip (pouting)
Angry	Skin between eyes creased Eyes narrowed or open wide	Lips pulled in tight Lips narrowed to a thin line
Scared	Eyebrows raised Eyes open wide Fast eye-blinking	Mouth slightly open
Surprised	Eyebrows raised Eyes open wide	Mouth slightly open
Disgusted	Eyebrows lowered Eyes narrowed	Nose wrinkled Raised upper lip

Get your child to look at you

The first step in helping your child to read your face is to get him to look at you. What if you just said, "Look at me"? Would that help? It might make your child look at you once, but if he doesn't find any value in looking at you, he's less likely to do it again on his own. So, first we'll talk about how to get your child to look at you. Later on in this chapter, we'll discuss how to make looking worthwhile for him.

The following pages will give you some ideas that you can use to **"hook your child to look."**

Hooks Get Looks

> Get face to face.

> Do the unexpected… then WAIT.

> Give things to your child bit by bit… then WAIT.

> Let things go wrong… then WAIT.

> Make mistakes on purpose… then WAIT.

> Say or do something about your child's interests… then WAIT.

Get face to face

Step one in getting your child to look at you is getting face to face. When you're face to face with your child, it's easier for him to look right into your eyes. So, give your child every opportunity to see your face "talk."

Pilar can't see Mom's face when they sit beside each other.

Pilar reacts to Mom's look of surprise because she sees her face.

It may not be easy to get face to face, but…

> If your child moves away from you, try to follow him to get face to face again.
> If he finds being face to face upsetting, try being beside him at first.
> If you are beside your child, lean forward so he can see your face.

It's hard to get play going when Mom and Ali are so far apart.

When Mom gets face to face with Ali, each of them can see what the other is interested in doing.

WAIT

Waiting is a powerful and simple hook to catch a child's attention. If you say or do something and then wait a few seconds longer than you normally would, your child may surprise you by looking right at you.

An important part of this strategy is that, while you wait, you look like you expect your child to respond to you. That means lean forward, raise your eyebrows and open your eyes wide. See the difference in what Ethan does when his mother waits in this way.

Last time we did this with your sister. Remember? She put all the macaroni on the floor. Then she walked all over it. Was I mad? I was so mad!

No waiting from Mom. So no looking or talking from Ethan.

Now, I'll wait.

Remember? Angie put all the macaroni on the floor!

... Angie walked all over the macaroni.

When Mom shows Ethan that she's waiting for a reply, he not only looks at her but replies happily.

You may have to force yourself to wait by counting slowly to 10 in your head. This will give your child a chance to figure out how you're feeling and how to respond.

As you'll learn over the next two pages, the simple strategy of waiting is even more powerful when combined with other strategies.

Do the unexpected...then WAIT

Children notice when things happen unexpectedly. If you change a familiar routine, your child will likely look at you to figure out what's going on. He'll search your face for clues.

Doing the unexpected means doing something you don't usually do. For instance, you can change your voice by talking either very loudly or very softly to get your child's attention. Or try something silly. Give him your shoes to wear when he's getting dressed, or offer him a drink when he doesn't have a glass to hold it. Then wait for his reaction.

Give things to your child bit by bit...then WAIT

Treats and toys that can be given a bit at a time can also be used to get your child's attention. If your child is used to your handing him these things all at once, he doesn't have much reason to look at you while you're doing it.

Surprise him, instead, by giving him just one little piece of apple or only one piece of a toy, such as one building block. Then wait for him to look at you to see what you're up to or to tell you he wants more.

Madison looks at Mom when she gets less juice than everyone else.

Let things go wrong...then WAIT

Every day, little things go wrong. Food falls on the floor, toys break and milk gets spilled. Instead of fixing these little problems right away, just wait. Your unusual behaviour might make your child curious enough to look for an explanation in your face.

Instead of turning on the water immediately, Dad waits for Matthew's reaction—and it works. Matthew looks at him and lets him know there's a problem.

Make mistakes on purpose...then WAIT

This fun strategy is also known as "Be creatively stupid!" Children love it when their parents make mistakes. Do something silly and your child will look at you to find out what's going on.

Try struggling to open a jar of jam—or try giving your child his sister's coat instead of his own—and wait for his reaction, saying nothing. Mispronounce or use silly words so that your child not only looks at you, but asks you what you said. Look how it works for Luis's mother.

Mom says the word the wrong way to get Luis's attention.

Say or do something about your child's interests... then WAIT

Your child will be more interested in looking at you if what *you* say or do is about something *he* has just said or done. Look at the difference in what Jose does in each of the pictures.

Did you play with Emily today?

Right now, Jose is interested in his truck, not in talking about Emily.

WHAM! That noise scared me!

Jose's mother talks about his interests and makes it fun for him to look at her face.

Highlight what you say without words

You've learned a few simple ways to get your child's attention. Here's another, easy-to-remember set of strategies: highlight what you say without words by using "the Four S's"—Say Less, Stress, Go Slow and Show. (In Chapter 5, we'll look at how you can use the Four S's to highlight your words.)

When you use the Four S's, your child will look at your body language and face more often. Even better, he'll realize that there's a lot of information in what you're not saying.

Say Less

You don't have to say a lot to get your child's attention. Consider how Jose's mother (on the previous page) got him to look at her by using a "fun word." When she says "Wham! That noise scared me!" the word "wham" stands out because Jose isn't used to hearing it. His mother waits after she says the word to give Jose a chance to shift his attention from the car to her. So "hook your child to look" by using attention-getting fun words like "wham," "yucky," "cool" and "wow."

When your child does look at you, give him an opportunity to concentrate on your nonverbal communication by using fewer words than usual. Too much talking might distract him from paying attention to your face.

What you say when your child looks should help him understand your facial expression—how you're feeling or what you're thinking. That's exactly what Jose's mother does when she tells him that the crashing sound of the car scared her.

Stress

It's not just what you say to your child that will grab his attention, but how you say it. Jose's mother uses a louder voice and adds a hand gesture when she says her fun word, "Wham!" So, to get your child to look at you, use a lively voice and actions to match.

To make sense of what they see, children use both what they see and what they hear. That means that you should exaggerate your happy, sad or scared voice to match the message on your face.

Go Slow

Many of our actions and facial expressions happen quickly. Try slowing down what you do when you're around your child. He'll have a better chance to read your body language and see what's happening on your face. That means letting your expression stay on your face longer than you usually would, so your child can take it in and think about what it means.

To help you slow down, try using a gesture along with your words, or by itself. For instance, point at your head or bang on it lightly as if to say, "What was I thinking?" Do it slowly to give your child the time he needs to understand.

Show

Your child will learn why it's important to look at you if you do something that will make his looking worthwhile. That doesn't mean giving him a candy or praise for looking. It means showing him that there's important information on your face about what you're thinking and how you feel.

Show or point to what you're talking about

Make sure that you draw attention to your face. Point to the part of your face that shows what's on your mind and tell your child what you're "saying" with your face. Remember that your child will need the most help in noticing your eyes.

Eric's mother draws his attention to her eyes and tells Eric what her eyes are "saying."

Show with actions, gestures and facial expressions

Exaggerate your actions, gestures and facial expressions so your child can easily understand them. For example, overdo frowning when something makes you unhappy, or turn your eyes into narrow slits to show anger.

Try letting your actions and face do all the talking sometimes. For example, when your child asks you if he can have a cookie, instead of saying yes, nod your head up and down and smile. Or shake your head for no. You can show him all of your feelings without ever saying a word.

The many ways you move your hands and body give your child extra information about how you're feeling. With time, your child may want to use the same gestures to get his messages across. So throw your hands in the air when you're happy or shrug your shoulders when you're confused. Sometimes, tell your child what you're doing and why you're doing it. (For example, "I'm wrinkling my nose because I don't like that smell.")

You can even teach your child how close to stand from people by showing him. Stand too close or too far when you talk to him, and then say something like, "Oh, I'm so far away. I'll move closer so you can see me better."

Show with pictures or videos

In photographs, things look different from the way they look in real life. Facial expressions, for instance, are frozen. In real life, the emotions we show on our faces change subtly and quickly.

For that reason, your child will benefit more from watching videos than looking at pictures. Turn down the sound and discuss the emotions that your child sees on the people's faces. Pause the video at emotional moments so your child has a chance to see the facial expressions frozen as well as in movement.

Specialized computer programs are also available that use actors to portray a variety of emotions in video clips. For example, one developed in Cambridge, England, is called "Mind Reading: The Interactive Guide to Emotions," available online.

Although moving images are generally better for this purpose, photographs and pictures in books can help, too. They give your child a chance to take his time studying faces and picking out key features. But keep in mind that recognizing facial expressions and body language in a book won't fully prepare your child to recognize them in a social situation.

Get Your Child to Follow Your Eyes

Following another person's eye gaze—looking where she looks—is an important part of socializing. When your child looks in the direction he sees you looking in, he's trying to figure out what's on your mind.

Let your eyes lead

To "let your eyes lead," first make it very clear what you're looking at. Your eyes should act like laser beams that point to what you're interested in. However, just looking at something might not give your child enough information. You might have to add some more obvious clues.

Look at how Mei's mother (on the next page) directs Mei to follow her eyes to a missing mitten. First she looks directly at the mitten and tells Mei that she sees it. When Mei needs some extra help to follow her mother's gaze, her mother not only looks but turns her whole body toward the mitten and points to it.

Mommy, I only have one mitten.

I think I know where the other one is.

First Mei's mother lets her eyes do the "talking."

When Mei doesn't follow her eyes to the missing mitten, her mother turns her body and points to it.

Play "eye games"

You want your child to see the value of watching your eyes. So try playing these games, which make following your eyes a lot of fun.

I Spy with My Little Eye

> Sit face to face with your child.
> Tell your child that you have a game to play called "I Spy with My Little Eye." Tell him that you see something in the room and you want him to find it.
> Pick something of a certain colour or something that begins with a specific letter.
> Say, "I spy with my little eye something that is blue" (or another colour), or "I spy with my little eye something that starts with a D" (or another letter).
> Stare at the object you want your child to look at.
> If looking alone doesn't work...
> Turn your body in the direction of the object.
> Point to the object.
> Put your arm close to the side of your child's head, so that he can look along your arm and beyond your pointing finger.
> Let your child take a turn being the one who "spies" something with his little eye.

Watch My Eyes and Find a Surprise

This game is adapted from one in Steven Gutstein's book *Relationship Development Intervention with Young Children* (2002).

> Begin the game by telling your child he is going to find some hidden objects.
> Tell your child that he will need to look at your eyes to find the objects.
> Show your child a few objects that you will hide. He will be more motivated if you hide small toys or treats that he can keep when he finds them.
> Have your child leave the room, or put a blindfold on him or ask him to close his eyes, while you hide the objects.
> Bring your child back into the room or have him take off the blindfold or open his eyes.
> Get face to face with your child.
> Tell your child: "Don't look for the toys (or treats) until I tell you to. You'll need to look at my eyes to find them."
> Make sure your child is looking at your eyes.
> In an exaggerated way, first look at your child with a big smile and then stare at where the first object is hidden.
> Now tell your child to start searching.
> If your child looks in the wrong place, immediately stop him and have him stand face to face with you (you should sit or kneel). Turn your head again toward the hidden object.
> If your child still can't "follow your eyes," turn your head and point to the correct spot, and then tell your child to search again.
> If your child can't follow your pointing, put your arm close to the side of your child's head, so that he can look along your arm and beyond your pointing finger.
> Once your child is successful, move on to the rest of the objects.
> Keep working on this activity until he can easily follow your eye gaze to the hidden objects.
> Then, let your child hide some things so he can use his eyes to help you find them.

You can make this game harder by being beside your child. If he doesn't look at your eyes, go back to the face-to-face position.

As your child searches, let him know how he's doing by telling him, "Look at my face and you'll know if you're getting close to the surprise." If your child is close to the hidden object, nod your head for yes. If he's not, shake your head for no.

Christopher doesn't realize his father is training him to follow his eyes when his father does it in a game.

More games

Playing games and singing songs face to face with your child gives him another way to focus on your face. Games like Simon Says, in which your child has to copy what you do, will help him focus on your body actions and face. In the game of Charades, your child has to guess the name of a movie or an emotion by watching someone else act it out without ever saying a word.

Simon says, open your eyes like this.

In a game of Simon Says, Alex has to watch his father carefully to play.

If you're mad and you know it, make a frown...

Sing songs that make your child look at your face.

Take familiar tunes and make up words or actions that will encourage your child to look at your face. For example, if you want your child to understand that looking at someone goes with listening to him, you might sing (to the tune of "Row, Row, Row Your Boat"), "Look, look, look at me. Look at me and listen." Or adapt the ever-popular song "If You're Happy and You Know It," as the mother shown here does.

Some board games and computer games are made to help your child learn to identify facial expressions. You can find these online or in most toy stores. They can be helpful, but remember that playing a computer game can't replace reading faces in real life.

. . . .

In this chapter you learned how to help your child understand other people's feelings and thoughts by reading their facial expressions, body language and tone of voice. By understanding more about what's on your mind, your child is starting to tune in to you. This is only the beginning, so let's move on. In Chapter 3, you'll see how understanding what we say without words is just one part of keeping a conversation going.

3

Get Ready for Conversation: "Break the ICE"

I wanted to play with Sarah today and she ran away.

Monster. I was pretending to be a scary monster.

What did you want to play, Josh?

People have conversations to connect with others—to share ideas and experiences. In the situation shown here, conversation opens the lines of communication between Josh and his mother. Through their conversation, Josh's mother discovers what has happened between Josh and Sarah.

This chapter will give you a clearer understanding of the rules of conversation—rules that most adults follow automatically—so you can pass them along to your child more effectively. For instance, each partner must take his or her turn at talking and listening. These turns must be taken at just the right time, with each turn connecting to the one before it. To do this, partners have to understand one another's feelings and thoughts.

After you read this part of the book, you'll have a better idea of what your child needs to learn about the basics of conversation.

What Makes a Good Conversation?

All of us have experienced good and bad conversations. We know we're in a good conversation when we feel involved, interested and valued by our conversation partner. We know we're in a bad conversation when we have stopped listening and are thinking about how to quickly get away from the person we're talking to.

Here's a conversation that's going nowhere. Neither woman has the slightest interest in what the other has to say.

Here's a conversation that's going somewhere. Each of the women is interested in what the other has to say.

Your child's ability to make friends also depends on his ability to have good conversations. Look at Anthony's approach to conversation:

Anthony breaks all of the rules of conversation.

Anthony asks Michael a lot of unrelated questions to try to start conversation. What he says sounds more like a "fact-finding mission" than a real conversation. He never gives Michael a chance to answer, and he makes him even more uncomfortable by standing too close. There's no mistaking how Michael feels. Notice how he steps back from Anthony. Now consider Jacob's approach, in the same situation:

Jacob follows all the rules of conversation.

Jacob's conversation with Michael goes much better than Anthony's. There are many reasons for this.

Jacob starts by showing an interest in Michael's action figure, then asks him to play and waits for an answer. When he notices Michael's reluctance to accept his invitation, Jacob makes a suggestion based on Michael's interests (action figures). That shows he cares about Michael's feelings. He stands just the right distance away from Michael and smiles.

Jacob has followed all of the basic conversational rules. Anthony has broken all of them. Consider the following list of conversation dos and don'ts.

> **What Successful Conversational Partners Do**
> > They say something and then wait for the other person to take his turn.
> > They listen to what the other person is saying and show their interest.
> > They comment on what the other person has just said—or they ask questions.
> > They try to understand how the other person thinks and feels.
>
> **What Successful Conversational Partners Don't Do**
> > They don't ask question after question.
> > They don't do all the talking—or all the listening.
> > They don't insist on talking only about one thing.

How Conversation Works

There are three stages to any conversation. First, there's the beginning, when one person initiates the conversation. Then comes the middle, when both partners continue the conversation. Finally, the end requires one person to bring the conversation to a close. During each stage of the conversation, both people have much to do—not just when they're speaking, but when they're listening, too.

Good conversation consists of three parts: **Initiate**, **Continue** and **End**—which you can remember as "**ICE**." To master conversation, your child needs to "break the ICE."

Initiate

Continue

End

Filling in the three checklists later in this chapter will help you figure out which part your child needs the most help with.

Ways to INITIATE conversations

How do people actually start a conversation? Sometimes we do it without words. For example, we get our listener's attention by looking him or her in the eye. Sometimes we smile. Of course, we use words, too. We can break the ice and begin the conversation with a standard greeting like, "Hi!" and follow with an easy-to-answer opening question, such as "How are you?" or "What's new?"

After we greet someone, we might make a comment to get the conversation going. There are many ways to do this. For instance, we could pay someone a compliment, say something about what that person is doing or tell the other person something interesting about ourselves.

Consider how Emily gets off to a good start with Daniel:

Emily knows that saying something nice about Daniel's tower is the best way to get herself an invitation to play.

Hey, Daniel. That's a cool tower!

Children can learn different ways to initiate conversations. Let's take a closer look at how Emily does it, both with and without words:

INITIATES WITH WORDS

Emily gets her friend's attention by using a greeting word ("Hey") and then saying his name (Daniel). Next, she gives Daniel a compliment ("That's a cool tower").

INITIATES WITHOUT WORDS

Emily stands near her friend, smiles and looks at him as she talks.

Ways to Initiate Conversations	
Without Words	**With Words**
> Use body actions, such as standing near the other person. > Look at the other person's face. > Smile at the other person. > Tap the other person on the shoulder. ... *and* wait for a response.	> Use a standard greeting. > Use the person's name. > Ask an easy-to-answer opening question, such as "How are you?" > Make a comment: • Give a compliment • Comment on what's happening • Share some information ... *and* wait for a response.

How does your child initiate conversation? Remember, the way your child initiates conversations with you and other adults can be very different from the way he initiates with other children. For example, he might say, "Hi! How are you?" to his grandmother but greet his friend with a high-five. We'll talk more about how children start conversations with other children in Chapter 10.

Using Conversation Checklist #1 below, decide how your child initiates conversation (or tries to initiate it).

Conversation Checklist #1

Initiating the Conversation

MY CHILD STARTS A CONVERSATION BY:	WITH WORDS	NEVER	SOMETIMES	OFTEN	WITHOUT WORDS	NEVER	SOMETIMES	OFTEN
Getting someone's attention	Says the person's name	○	○	○	Stands near the person	○	○	○
					Looks at the person's face	○	○	○
					Taps the person on the shoulder	○	○	○

Example of how my child gets someone's attention:

Greeting someone	E.g., "Hi"	○	○	○	Faces the person	○	○	○
					Smiles at the person	○	○	○

Example of how my child greets someone:

Asking an opening question	"Hi. How are you?"	○	○	○	Looks at the person and waits for an answer	○	○	○
	"Hi. What's your name?"	○	○	○				
	"What are you doing?"	○	○	○				

Example of some opening questions my child uses:

Saying something nice	Gives a compliment, e.g., "Cool truck!"	○	○	○	Looks at the person when he says something nice and and then waits	○	○	○

Example of what my child says/does:

Conversation Checklist #1 continued

MY CHILD STARTS A CONVERSATION BY:	WITH WORDS	NEVER	SOMETIMES	OFTEN	WITHOUT WORDS	NEVER	SOMETIMES	OFTEN
Talking about something that happened in the past	E.g., "I went to the zoo."	○	○	○	Looks at the person and then waits	○	○	○
Example of what my child says/does:								
Talking about something that will happen in the future	E.g., "I'm going to go to camp."	○	○	○	Looks at the person and and then waits	○	○	○
Example of what my child says/does:								
Asking another about feelings, likes/dislikes	"Are you having fun?"	○	○	○	Looks at the person and then waits	○	○	○
	"What do you like to play?"	○	○	○				
Example of what my child says/does:								

Ways to CONTINUE conversations

Once we've broken the ice by saying hello and asking an easy-to-answer question or making a comment, we have to keep the conversation going. Continuing a conversation means each person takes turns, with and without words.

Sometimes a continuing turn might only be a "filler," something we say— like "uh-huh" or "mmm"—just to let the other person know we're listening or agreeing. Most of the time, we continue conversations by answering and asking questions, making comments and looking interested when the other person talks.

To keep a conversation going, speaker and listener must stay tuned in to one another so each can connect his turn to the one before.

On the next page, take a look at how James and his mother keep their conversation going.

James's mom asks a question that she knows will interest James, and James is ready with his answer.

James follows his mother's comment with one of his own on the same topic.

Both James and his mother use a comment followed by a question to keep their conversation going.

Consider how James continues the conversation both with and without words:

CONTINUES WITH WORDS
James answers his mother's questions and makes a comment about wanting to be a big, scary pumpkin. James asks his own question ("Do you think they have a pumpkin costume at the mall?").

CONTINUES WITHOUT WORDS
Both James and his mother look and smile at each other while they talk and listen.

Ways to Continue Conversations	
Without Words	**With Words**
> Use body actions, such as standing near the other person. > Look at the other person's face when listening. > Smile when listening. > Nod head when listening. … *and* wait for a response.	> Answer questions. > Comment on what the other person says. > Ask a question that is on topic. > Ask for clarification ("What do you mean?" or "I don't understand"). > Use fillers ("uh-huh," "mm-hmm," "yeah," "okay," "right"). … *and* wait for a response.

How does your child continue conversations? Is he better at continuing conversations with words or without words? Does he respond to your comments with a comment of his own? Or does he only respond to questions that he knows need an answer?

Do your conversations often break down because your child doesn't know how to continue taking his turn? Conversations can break down for a lot of different reasons. Sometimes your child may miss the general idea of the conversation. He may take a turn which is not really on the same subject as your turn, as Anthony does in the illustration below.

Five-year-old Anthony and his father are talking about an upcoming class trip.

So, your class is going to visit the fire station tomorrow.

That guy always bugs me.

It sounds like Anthony's missed the general idea of the conversation. Maybe he's thinking about how his friend Brian, who has been mean to him in the past, might treat him at the fire station.

Can I get you a drink to start?

Uh…I eat macaroni.

In the picture to the right, Gracie also has trouble continuing a conversation with her dad, but for a different reason.

Gracie can't keep the conversation going because she doesn't understand her father's question.

Using the Conversation Checklist #2 below, decide how your child continues conversations, or tries to continue them.

Conversation Checklist #2

Continuing the Conversation

MY CHILD CONTINUES A CONVERSATION BY:	WITH WORDS	NEVER	SOMETIMES	OFTEN	WITHOUT WORDS	NEVER	SOMETIMES	OFTEN
Responding to another person's greeting	Says "hello" back	○	○	○	Turns toward the person	○	○	○
					Looks at the person when responding	○	○	○
Example of what my child says/does:								
Answering yes/no questions	Says "yes" or "no"	○	○	○	Shakes his head	○	○	○
Example of what my child says/does:								
Answering questions: (What is it? Who? Where?)	E.g., "What is your favourite video?" Child answers, "*Shrek.*" Or, "What are you doing?" Child answers, "Playing computer."	○	○	○	Looks at person asking question	○	○	○
Example of what my child says/does:								
Repeating what someone says	Using the same words	○	○	○	Looks at person	○	○	○
Example of what my child says/does:								
Making a comment about what the other person said	E.g., "My favourite video is Spiderman too."/"Me too."	○	○	○	Looks at person	○	○	○
					Waits	○	○	○
Example of what my child says/does:								

Conversation Checklist #2 continued

MY CHILD CONTINUES A CONVERSATION BY:	WITH WORDS	NEVER	SOMETIMES	OFTEN	WITHOUT WORDS	NEVER	SOMETIMES	OFTEN
Asking the person a question about what they said	E.g. (after child says he goes to such and such a school), "What is your teacher's name?"	○	○	○	Looks at person	○	○	○
					Waits	○	○	○

Example of what my child says/does:

Letting the other person know that he doesn't understand something said	E.g., "What do you mean?" or "I don't understand."	○	○	○	Looks at person	○	○	○
					Waits	○	○	○

Example of what my child says/does:

Showing he's listening to what the other person is saying	E.g., uses fillers like "uh-huh," "yes," "OK," "me too"	○	○	○	Nods head, looks interested, then waits	○	○	○
					Looks at the person talking	○	○	○

Example of what my child says/does:

Introducing a new topic appropriately	With a comment or a question	○	○	○	Looks at person	○	○	○

Example of what my child says/does:

Clarifying what he said	E.g., tries saying something again	○	○	○	Shows the other person what he means with gestures	○	○	○
	Gives more details to help explain	○	○	○				

Example of what my child says/does:

Figuring out if the listener is happy, sad, bored or confused	E.g., "Are you listening?"	○	○	○	Looks at person's face and body language	○	○	○

Example of what my child says/does:

Ways to END conversations

We end conversations after both people have finished talking to one another or one person wants to do something else. To end at the right time, we depend on the nonverbal messages we send and receive. For example, when a neighbour looks at her watch or glances away, it might be because she wants the conversation to end.

To bring the conversation to a close, we rely on some tried-and-true closings, such as, "I've got to go now. Bye!" or "Thanks for your time." As with greetings, closings often follow a predictable pattern.

Look at how Mitchell ends the conversation, both with and without words:

Mitchell knows how to end his play date. His mother reminds him about the important part he forgets.

Mitchell ends the conversation with words as well as wordless messages:

ENDS WITH WORDS
Mitchell tells Mark that he's leaving ("Gotta go") and ends his conversation with a tried-and-true closing remark ("See you later").

ENDS WITHOUT WORDS
Mitchell waves to Mark and smiles as he ends their conversation.

Ways to End Conversations

Without Words	With Words
> Look away when trying to end. > Stand up. > Wave goodbye. > Smile and look at other person saying "goodbye." > Point to where you are going. … *and* wait for a response.	> Say you're going. > Say something nice (such as "I had fun"). > Use a tried-and-true closing, sometimes with the person's name ("Bye, Mark" or "See you later, Sarah"). … *and* wait for a response.

How does your child end conversations? Children who have difficulty with social communication often don't formally end their conversations. They just get up and walk away. If that's what your child does, you can help him learn to finish in a more sociable way. Possibly, your child knows some tried-and-true closings but doesn't use them when he's supposed to.

Complete Conversation Checklist #3 below to decide how your child ends conversations, or tries to end them.

Conversation Checklist #3

E

Ending the Conversation

MY CHILD ENDS A CONVERSATION BY:	WITH WORDS	NEVER	SOMETIMES	OFTEN	WITHOUT WORDS	NEVER	SOMETIMES	OFTEN
Telling the listener he has to go	E.g., "I'm finished now," "Gotta go," "I don't want to read this book any more."	○	○	○	Puts toys etc. away	○	○	○
					Looks at person	○	○	○

Example of what my child says/does:

Saying something about what's going to happen	"I'm going to play cars now."	○	○	○	Points or gestures to what he's going to do next	○	○	○

Example of what my child says/does:

Conversation Checklist #3 continued

MY CHILD ENDS A CONVERSATION BY:	WITH WORDS	NEVER	SOMETIMES	OFTEN	WITHOUT WORDS	NEVER	SOMETIMES	OFTEN
Saying something about the next time together	"See you later."	◯	◯	◯	Smiles and looks at other person	◯	◯	◯
Example of what my child says/does:								
Using a tried-and-true closing	"Bye."	◯	◯	◯	Waves and smiles	◯	◯	◯
					Looks at other person	◯	◯	◯
Example of what my child says/does:								
Using a tried-and-true closing with someone's name	"Bye, Jonah."	◯	◯	◯	Waves and smiles	◯	◯	◯
Example of what my child says/does:								

After reading this chapter, you might feel there are so many things that your child can't do. But to move on, look at what he or she can do.

The Conversational Checklists should help you identify your child's strengths and show you how to build on the turns he is already taking. For example, if your child is responding to your questions but not asking any of his own, you know that he has the idea that questions and answers go together. That means he's ready to ask you something.

The next chapter tells you how to take your child one step further in conversations by modelling what successful conversational partners do.

4

Use Your "I-Cues" for Better Conversations

If you've figured out what conversational skills your child already has, you're ready to help him have longer and more interesting conversations. One of the hardest skills for him to learn will be keeping a conversation going, and there's no better person to learn it from than you.

Your child's conversations with you give him his most important early learning experiences. Every time you have a conversation with him, he has an example of how a conversation works. As he learns more about conversations, he'll use what he's learned from you in his conversations with other children.

In this chapter you'll find out how to give your child just the right amount of help so that he can learn first-hand that keeping conversation going makes everyday life more fun.

Conversation Basics

This chapter's main topic is keeping conversations going. But before we move forward, let's review two fundamentals of conversation that were introduced in earlier chapters and learn about a new one: using routines.

Make use of routines

For children who are inexperienced in conversation, daily routines such as dinnertime or bedtime are good places to start. These shared times occur day after day in much the same way. Since many routines are so familiar to your child, it's possible to have his undivided attention at these times. Having a conversation when your child is doing something else, like playing with toys, is more challenging.

Family meals present many common topics of conversation because everyone is eating the same food and discussing the day's events together. Mealtimes also encourage turn-taking by providing a predictable structure: setting the table, eating, talking about what's happening and about each person's day, and clean-up.

Think of all of the words that your child hears over and over at mealtimes: "Please pass the salt/water/juice (etc.)," "Thank you," "You're welcome," "How's the food?" "Do you want more?" "I'm finished" and so on. Mealtimes also give your child repeated opportunities to hear the tried-and-true openings and endings that will help him in all his conversations, such as "How was your day?" and "See you later."

Bedtime is also prime time for conversation. When you tuck your child into bed at night, he might want to prolong the good-night routine with conversation. While he's in the mood, talk together about what happened during the day or about the book you've just read. Dim the lights first and make sure there are no distractions.

Follow your child's lead

Beyond daily routines, generally the best time for a conversation with your child is any time he feels like talking. He'll probably be more ready to talk, for instance, when something happens that interests him.

In this chapter you're going to learn how you can build on your child's interests to help him take his turn in the conversation. As you learned in Chapter 1, the best way to help your child take his turn is to be more responsive in conversation by following his lead. This chapter will show you many strategies to help you be more responsive, all of them involving the key concept of waiting.

Wait... and wait some more!

By waiting, you let your child know that you are expecting a response from him. But even more importantly, you also give him enough time to respond to what you say. Children with social communication challenges, such as those with HFA or AS, often understand the turn-taking pattern of conversations. However, they need more time before they're ready to take their turn.

Perhaps your child takes longer to make sense of or "process" what you just said to him. He might be daydreaming or unsure of what he should say next. There could also be sensory distractions, such as noise or a pattern on the ceiling that has grabbed his attention. Your child may even stop in the middle of what he's saying because he's having trouble finding the right word.

All of this means that you'll have to wait a bit longer than you usually would for him to respond. Most people wait only about one second when their conversation partner doesn't respond, and then they take another turn. But when you're talking to your child, it's important to try to wait between five and ten seconds before talking again.

While you wait, let your face and body language show that you're expecting him to reply. Count silently to yourself if waiting isn't easy for you. Five seconds is a lot longer than you may think.

When Mom waits, Ethan surprises her by guessing what's for dessert and making a joke.

Use Your "I-Cues" to Keep the Conversation Going

"I-Cues" are a set of skills for you to use whenever you talk to your child. The I's will help you follow your child's lead so that you are responsive to him all the time. The Cues signal to your child that the next turn in the conversation is his.

The I's...

> **Include** your child's interests, ideas and words
> **Interpret** his message
> **Introduce** your own ideas
> **Insist** on a change of topic

...help you take your turn.

The Cues...

> **Comment**... and wait
> **Ask a question**... and wait
> **Make it easier to answer your question**... and wait
> **Hint**... and wait
> **Make a suggestion**... and wait
> **Tell your child what to say or do**... and wait

...tell your child that it's his turn.

Use the I's to Take Your Turn

First, let's look at the four I's: Include, Interpret, Introduce and Insist. They'll help you find the responsive style you need for better conversations with your child.

Include your child's interests, ideas and words

"Saying something about your child's interests" was one of the "hooks" we talked about in Chapter 2 to get your child to look at you. You can use the same principle to keep him interested in conversation.

To show your child that his interests, feelings and ideas matter to you, start your end of the conversation by talking about what he's interested in at the moment. By starting with what your child is interested in right now, you'll also make sure that you're both focused on the same topic.

For example, Brady has just finished watching his favourite TV show, so his father begins the conversation like this: "Hi, Brady. What were you watching?" Look at how the conversation takes off when Dad starts with Brady's interests:

By talking about what Brady is interested in, Dad makes it easier and more fun for them to have a conversation.

A simple way to connect your turn to your child's turn is to use his words to reflect back what he says (as Dad does in the illustration above, when he starts his reply with the word "feathers"). By including the words he has just said, you can show him that you have heard and accepted his message. He'll feel powerful and important when he hears you using his words. It will also help him pay attention to you.

Now and then, you can include your child's words simply by agreeing or disagreeing with what he says. For example, if your child says, "I like this story," you can respond, "I like this story, too."

 ## *Interpret* his messages

Sometimes, you can't use your child's words because you're not sure what he's saying. That's when the best way to be responsive is to act as an "interpreter."

Interpreting your child's message means putting into words what you think your child is trying to tell you with his gestures, actions and even words. By expressing his point of view in words, you are letting him know that you're listening, watching him and trying to understand what he's telling you.

For example, if your child pushes broccoli off his plate at dinner, he's probably telling you "I won't eat this." So, as he's refusing the food, interpret and say something like "You don't want broccoli." If he stands next to another child and watches him playing a game, he probably wants to join in the game. In this situation you could interpret by saying, "You want to play that game, too."

When you interpret for your child what other people around the two of you are doing, especially in social situations, you help him understand the meaning behind their actions. For example, if your child is talking to someone who is looking at his watch, you might interpret that person's action by saying, "It's time to go. Mr. Goodman has to work."

Interpreting also comes in handy when your child says something incorrectly. For instance, he may use the wrong word, or he may say a few words instead of a whole sentence. Then, if he can't correct himself, you'll need to figure out what his meaning is and expand on what he's said or fix it up.

Luke's mom interprets for him by putting what he's trying to say into a complete sentence.

When you interpret the meaning behind your child's actions, you might also want to show him what he could say if he were to use words. To do this, first interpret his actions from his point of view: "You don't want broccoli." Then give him a model of what he could say by adding your own point of view: "I want broccoli." It doesn't matter if your point of view is different from your child's. What matters is that your child has a chance to hear sentences similar to ones that he can use another time.

Mom interprets from her child's point of view and then adds her own.

Introduce your own ideas

You can add new and interesting ideas to the conversation with your own comments. Your comments can keep the interaction going by building on what your child is doing, saying or seems to be interested in. For instance, if your child likes to name the capitals of countries, you can tell him something new about these cities. ("In Ottawa, people skate on the river in the winter.")

Introducing your own ideas is much more than just a way to keep the conversation going. Sometimes, as parents, we make comments that we don't expect a response to. We're just interested in giving our child a new idea to think about. The next two chapters in this book will suggest many ideas you can share with your child—ideas that will open up his mind to the world around him.

It's not always best to let your child lead the conversation. Sometimes, letting your child lead will take you both into a conversational dead end. This can happen when your child gets stuck talking about one thing and can't move on. If he's not tuned in to you, he thinks that since he's passionate about something, you must be, too.

For example, every time Eric gets in his mother's car, he insists on talking about the electronic buttons. When his mother follows his lead by including his interests in their conversation, it sounds a bit like Eric is doing research on the car's wiring instead of having a real conversation. His mother wants to talk about what he did at school that day—anything other than buttons.

Eric only wants to talk about the car's buttons.

To break Eric's repetitive pattern of talking about the car buttons, his mother might find a way to expand on Eric's interests by adding some new ideas. For example, she could talk about what cars were like before buttons opened and shut windows and controlled the lights.

If, however, Eric stays interested only in the buttons, his mother will have to introduce a brand new topic. It will be easier for him to switch topics if the new one is just as interesting as the old one.

Getting Eric to forget about the buttons takes some quick thinking on his mother's part. She links the old topic (the buttons) with the new topic (reading one of Eric's favourite books).

Keep in mind that, even when you lead your child away from his favourite topic, there's another reason why he might not follow your lead. If your child abruptly changes the topic of a conversation to one he's more familiar with, it's possible that he hasn't understood what you've said. He might be trying to keep the conversation going by talking about something he knows a lot about.

Mom's conversation is too complicated for Emily to understand. So instead of responding, Emily lists all the things she remembers seeing at the toy store.

When your child keeps returning to what he wants to talk about because your conversation confuses him, clarify what you've said. Use the Four S's: Say Less 😊 by simplifying complicated sentences, Stress ❤️ key words, Go Slow 🐢 when you talk and Show 👆 your child what you mean with actions or a picture.

First we'll pack.
Then let's go to the toy store.
We'll buy Abby a present.

Abby likes dolls.

When Mom breaks her long sentence into three shorter ones and shows Emily a picture, the conversation gets back on track.

If your child understands you and still wanders off-topic for other reasons, interpret for him and then remind him what the conversation was about before. ("You're thinking about your computer game. Right now, we're talking about visiting Grandma.")

 Insist on a change of topic

If, no matter what you try, your child persists in talking about his own interests, you'll have to be more direct. You'll have to insist on a change of topic. Warn your child that, after a few moments, you're planning to have a conversation about something else. Then switch topics.

Mom insists on a topic change but prepares Eric for it gently.

Eric, let's talk about one more button.
Then we're going to talk about school.

You can help your child "see" how much longer he has before he needs to move on to a new topic by using a timer. Or you can try using a visual cue, such as a card that shows your child the number of things he can still say about something before his time on this subject is up. ("Let's say two more things about the buttons and then talk about something else.") You might also work out a signal that you send to your child to warn him that it's time to change the topic, such as holding your hand up in the stop position.

This sort of warning works well, not only during conversations, but at other times, too. When your child is stuck doing or saying the same thing over and over, give him a friendly warning that there's going to be a change. ("One more slide and then let's try the ropes.")

> You will rarely respond to your child just by using one of the I's on its own. Most of the time you'll combine two or three of them. For example, you might first interpret ("You really love computers") and then introduce your own idea ("I think you like books, too").

Use the Cues to Show Your Child It's His Turn

Once you've begun using the four I's—especially by including his interests, interpreting his message and introducing your own ideas—your conversations with your child might start to flow quite naturally. However, he might need an extra nudge to take his turn. The Cues discussed below should give you some new ideas about how you can signal to him that it's his turn to say or do something.

Make a comment... and wait

One of the best and most natural Cues to use with your child in conversation is a comment about what he's interested in at the moment or what he has just said. Adding new, related ideas to the conversation, these comments encourage your child to take another turn in the conversation.

Your comments let you share new information about the world. ("Dinosaurs are extinct. That means they don't live on earth any more.") They also let your child know how others are thinking and feeling. ("I like the stegosaurus best.") As we saw in Chapter 3, you can use a comment to start a conversation, to continue one or to end one.

If your comment interests your child and you wait expectantly, he might respond with a comment of his own. Waiting expectantly means that you open your eyes wide, raise your eyebrows and lean forward.

Comments can set off a chain reaction, cueing your child to respond. Dad's comment (on page 53) about Brady's interest in dinosaurs with feathers

("I thought they had scales") does just that. After he makes it, Brady feels like sharing some more of his own interesting information with his father ("Some of them had feathers and they could fly").

Comments don't have to be long and involved. You can use a filler, such as "uh-huh," "yeah?" or "really?" to encourage your child to continue talking. Or simply repeat what your child has said, sounding interested in hearing more. For example, if your child says, "The dog chased him," you could look interested and say something like, "The dog chased him. Oh, no!"

When Dad sounds interested, Mark tells more of his story.

Compliments, Polite Words, Openers and Closers
Most of your comments will be spontaneous and follow naturally from what your child has just said. However, some of the things that you say most often will be automatic and repetitive. These include your use of compliments (such as "I like your picture" or "Well done!"), standard polite words ("Please," "Thank you," "I think so, too," "Sorry") and tried-and-true openers and closers ("Bye," "See you later"). The repetitiveness, though, is helpful for a child who likes learning this way. And hearing some key phrases over and over will help him acquire the courteous speech most people expect to hear.

Ask a question . . . and wait

Comments don't always elicit a response. If your child doesn't respond to your comment, ask a question and wait for him to respond. Sometimes all your child needs is for you to say, "And then what happened?"

Asking questions is a natural way to keep your child involved in the conversation. Parents use questions a lot because children respond naturally to the upward voice inflection that comes at the end of questions.

Questions vary in their difficulty and their purpose. If you are aware of how difficult certain kinds of questions can be for your child to answer, then you can choose them more carefully.

Open questions:

> **What happened?**
> **Wh- questions + "thought" words**
> **How?**
> **Why?**

Open questions ask for a long answer. For example, it's hard for your child to answer the question "What happened at school today?" with a single word.

Open questions can also ask for more imaginative answers that make your child think about more than just the facts. Questions of this kind may encourage your child to problem-solve ("What could you do about it?"), to give opinions ("What might happen if...?") or to talk about his emotions ("How do you feel about...?").

To encourage your child to think about what others are thinking, try Wh- questions (starting with "who," "what," "when" or "where") plus thought words. Some examples: "What does he think about...?" "Who do you think Grandma will want at her birthday?" "Where does Daddy think we are?" "When did she think the toy broke?"

"How" and "why" questions also require long and thoughtful answers. Questions beginning with "how"—such as "How do you make playdough?"—look for an explanation of how something is done. "Why" questions almost always make your child think about the reason someone does or feels something. (In Chapter 5, we'll spend more time looking at how open questions help your child think.)

Why are you so sad, Katie?

I want to swing, too.

When Mom asks Katie a question beginning with "why," Katie has a chance to sort out her feelings.

Closed Wh- questions:

> **What?**

> **Who?**

> **Where?**

> **When?**

Closed Wh- questions are not as hard as open questions for your child to answer. Questions that ask for facts—like "What do you want to eat?" "Who's that?" and "Where are you going?"—can often be answered with just one word or a short phrase. For that reason, these questions are often good ways to keep your child in the conversation. They show him that you're interested in what he thinks, without asking too much from him.

If, however, you ask your child too many questions of this kind, he might feel pressured to come up with the "right" answer. Then, conversation may seem like just a test instead of a back-and-forth sharing of ideas.

When Mom asks too many questions, Emily doesn't feel like answering any of them.

> What did you eat at Grandma's? …
> Who did you play ball with? …
> What movie did you watch?

Easy-to-answer questions:

> **Yes-or-no questions**

> **Choice questions**

> **Frequently asked questions**

> **Fill-in-the-blank questions**

The easiest questions of all to answer, in general, are the ones in this group. These questions allow your child to take a turn and stay in the conversation by responding with a single word or short phrase.

Among the simplest questions are those that ask for a yes-or-no answer ("Do you like juice?"). Yes-or-no questions also include the tag-ons like "don't you?" and "didn't he?" that turn comments into questions ("He walked a long way, didn't he?"). Choice questions call on the listener to make a choice ("Do you want the red one or the green one?"). And when it comes to frequently asked questions (such as "How are you?"), the answers can be so familiar that we've actually memorized them ("Fine, thanks").

Did William give you his guitar?

Are you playing rock or rap?

Yes.

Rock and roll.

Mom uses two kinds of easy-to-answer questions. First she asks Ben a yes-or-no question and then a choice question to keep him in the conversation.

If your child has difficulty answering any question, try the fill-in-the-blank method. That means that you begin to answer the question yourself and then wait for your child to complete the sentence ("What does Tom like?" "Tom likes pizza and…?").

I'm making your favourite food. What do you think it is?

Macaroni and…?

Huh?

Cheese! Yay!

When Kevin can't answer his mother's first question, she lets him "fill in the blank."

Make it easier to answer your question… and wait

After asking your child a question, wait expectantly for him to answer. If your child ignores the question, can't answer or gives an answer that doesn't fit with the question, you have a few options. You can give your child more information (hints) and then re-ask the question. You can ask an easier question. You can answer the question yourself, so your child learns how answers follow questions. Or you can help your child fix up his answer (if his answer doesn't make sense).

Let's look at how each of these cues might work to help your child continue the conversation.

Give your child hints and then ask again

Sometimes a subtle hint or two does the trick. In the picture shown here, Shaquille's mother tries to have a conversation with him about his day with his aunt. When Shaquille can't answer her question about what movie he saw, notice how she gives more information and re-asks the question to help him respond.

> What movie *did you* and Aunt Michelle see today?

> I think it was about a fish. What was it called?

> Huh?

> *Finding Nemo.* Nemo got lost and was trying to get home.

When Shaquille can't answer her first question, Mom gives him a hint and then asks again. It's just what Shaquille needs to join the conversation.

Ask an easier question

When you think your question might have been too difficult for your child, try a question he can answer more easily. If, for example, he can't answer an open question ("Who do you think will be at Grandma's house?"), try asking him a closed question. That might mean offering him a choice ("Do you think Uncle Robert or Chantelle will be there?") or asking a yes-or-no question ("What about Chantelle? Will she be there?").

Answer the question yourself

If your child doesn't understand or needs to be reminded that questions are followed by answers, answering the question yourself is an option. When Claire doesn't respond to her father's question, he shows her that his question needs an answer by giving it himself.

> Can you make the bunny hop?...

> I can make him hop.

When Claire doesn't answer, her father takes her turn for her.

Help your child fix up his answer

When your child gives the wrong answer, bring it to his attention and find out what he means. This works when you want to help your child find the right words or when he doesn't give you enough information.

When Brad can't find the right word, Mom makes him think about what he's said by exaggerating his mistake.

 ## Avoid questions that stop conversations

Questions can help your child continue the conversation, but don't overdo it. Too many questions can turn your child off, especially if he feels you've got a "right answer" in mind and you're just waiting for him to say it. So, balance the number of questions you use with an equal number of comments. Avoid:

> Asking too many questions
> Asking questions...
   • that test what your child knows
   • that your child doesn't have time to answer
   • that are too hard for your child to answer

> **Remember:** Children usually need a lot of practice answering questions before they ask their own.

 ## *Hint*... and wait

Another way to get your child to take a turn in the conversation is to try being subtle by dropping a hint. A hint is a general comment that gives your child an idea of what he could do or say next. For example, to get your child to tell you what he likes to eat, you might hint by saying, "I think you like pizza, too."

After hinting, look expectant so your child knows that you expect him to do or say something.

To pick up on a hint, your child must have the ability to guess at your intentions. If he can't do that yet, you'll have to give him a more straightforward Cue.

Make a suggestion… and wait

Suggestions are more specific than hints, but they still don't tell your child exactly what to do or say. Often, your suggestions will begin with "You could" or "You can" followed by your expectation for your child. For example, if you want your child to talk about his favourite TV show, you might make the suggestion, "You could tell me something about that show."

When Alex can't answer Mom's question, she gives him a hint. But Alex needs more help, so Mom makes a suggestion.

Tell your child what to say or do … and wait

As a last resort, you can tell your child exactly what to say. That means that you give him the words just as you expect him to repeat them ("Ask Daddy, 'Are we going to walk Fido?'"). Or give him specific directions on what to do ("Stand closer to me so I can hear you").

This cue is useful when your child has no idea what's expected. Remember, however, that directing your child too often might get him to take his turn but will also make him more dependent on you.

Choosing Your Cues
Here's a general rule for figuring out when to use the Cues discussed in this chapter. Give as little help as possible to get your child to continue. If that doesn't work, give more help as needed.

> Make a comment.   ▲ LEAST HELP
> Ask a question.
> Make it easier to answer your question.
> Hint.
> Make a suggestion.
> Tell your child what to say or do.   ▼ MOST HELP

Don't forget to WAIT after each Cue!

Give Visual Cues

If your child is a visual learner, it might be worth making a few cue cards to remind him what to say. On individual cards or a large piece of paper, draw some pictures and write a few key words, phrases or sentences.

Keep your cue cards simple.

Cue cards can give your child a script for his conversations, such as ideas for some compliments and conversation openers and closers. For example, a cue card can prompt your child to say, "Hi! I like your..." or "I'm sorry." Cue cards can also remind your child about some of the rules of conversation.

If you don't have time to make cue cards ahead of time, try writing (if your child can read) or drawing them as you need them. That means when you see your child struggling to find the right thing to say, take out a pen and paper and write out something he can use in the situation, such as, "I don't understand" or "I don't want to play now."

You can use cue cards before, during or after your conversation with your child. Before your conversation or activity, use cue cards to rehearse what your child can do and say. During the activity, place the card where your child can see it and point to it when your child gets stuck. After the activity, use the cue cards to review with your child what went well.

· ·

In this chapter, you learned how following your child's lead by using your I's can help you have a two-way conversation with him. In particular this means including his interests and interpreting his actions and the actions of others. When your child gets stuck on one idea, however, you can't always follow his lead. To help him move on, you can introduce a new topic. And if you have to, insist that he find something else to talk about.

Getting your child to take his own turn in conversations won't always be easy. He will need Cues to let him know when it's his turn to continue and what that turn could be. Your comments, questions, hints, suggestions, instructions and even little messages you write on paper will remind him when and how to hold up his end of the conversation.

The next step to being a good conversational partner is for your child to understand more than just the words. To have a truly successful conversation, your child has to understand the thoughts and feelings of his conversational partner. Keep reading to find out how to help your child do more than just take his turn at the right time.

Conversation Tip Sheet

Here's a tip sheet for you and your child. We'll talk more about how to use it in the following chapters, especially in Chapter 11.

How to Initiate Conversations

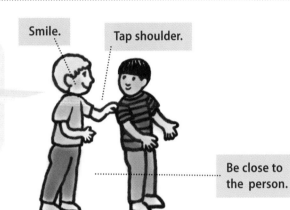

Smile.

Tap shoulder.

Say "Hi" and ask the person's name.

Ask an easy question:
"How are you?"
"What are you doing?"
"How was your day?"

Be close to the person.

How to Continue Conversations

Ask a question: "What kind of apples do you like?"

Answer question:
"I only like the red ones with the points on the bottom."

Say something about what the person said: "Those are called Delicious apples."

How to End Conversations

Say you're going:
"I have to go home now."
"Gotta go."
"I want to watch TV now."

Use a tried-and-true closing + person's name:
"See you tomorrow, Jason."

Help Your Child Tune In to Others

Every day, what you do and how you act depends a lot on what you think others are thinking. For example, if Brady, the boy in the picture above, knows that his sister is sad because she hasn't got the bicycle she was hoping for, he can make her feel better. In turn, his sister might give him a hug or let him play with her toys. Empathy, or being able to put yourself in another person's head, is at the heart of all successful relationships.

In this chapter, you'll learn more about what you can do to help your child tune in to other people's thoughts and feelings. He'll find it easier to have conversations and build relationships if he can learn to see things from the other person's point of view.

Understanding That "You" and "I" Think Differently

To really appreciate the thoughts of others, your child has to see the difference between himself and someone else. In other words, he has to understand that there are two sides to every story. Two people don't always want the same things, know the same things or hold the same opinions. Children must understand this before they can begin to grasp what's going on in the minds of others.

The ability to understand that other people's thoughts and feelings differ from our own is sometimes called "theory of mind." We call it a theory because no person can ever know exactly what's going on in someone else's head.

Many common English expressions describe this basic ability. "Tuning in" to others is just one. "Being on the same page," "standing in someone else's shoes," "reading a person's mind" and "he knows me like a book" are a few more.

In Chapter 2, you read about all the things a child can do when he learns to read people's faces and body language. He can understand how people feel. He can understand the meaning behind words people say. He can predict what people will do. And he can respond sensitively to people, based on their messages.

But useful as these skills are, they're limited without the basic insights and vocabulary that let us really tune in to others. Read on to learn how to help your child take his first steps in this direction.

Liam is starting to tune in to what's going on in his big brother's mind. He isn't sure whether he should believe him because he knows how his mother feels about watching TV, and he knows how much his brother wants to watch TV.

Stages of Tuning In

The ability to understand other people doesn't happen all at once. It takes about six years for most children, beginning in the first year of life, to become completely tuned in to other people. Your child might take eight or ten years, or even longer. It may be something he always has to work extra hard at.

But no matter how many years it takes him, your child's understanding of others will pass through a series of five stages. These stages are the same ones, more or less, that every child must go through. Knowing what they are will give you an idea of what your child needs to learn to progress to the next stage.

Thinking everyone likes the same things you do causes problems in relationships.

Stage 1: Understanding wanting

Every child's first lesson about wanting is that other people sometimes want things that are different from what he wants. Toddlers learn this simple truth when their desires conflict with those of their parents. (For instance, they want to eat candy and their parents won't let them.)

Sometime after a child has begun to understand what other people want, he can start predicting their actions and feelings. Then he can use this information to figure out how to react to them.

A child who has reached Stage 1 has learned these ideas (usually in the order shown):

> Different people want different things.
> To get what they want, people act in different ways.
> When people get what they want, they feel happy.
> When people don't get what they want, they feel unhappy.

In Stage 1, a child understands and talks about what people want.

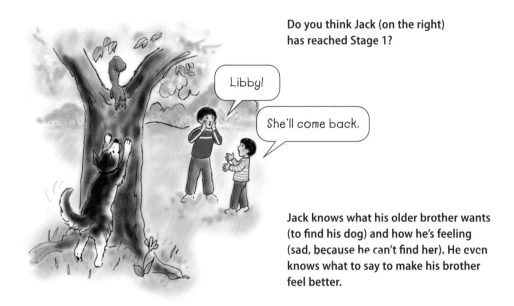

Do you think Jack (on the right) has reached Stage 1?

Libby!

She'll come back.

Jack knows what his older brother wants (to find his dog) and how he's feeling (sad, because he can't find her). He even knows what to say to make his brother feel better.

Stage 2: Understanding thinking

When we think (or know, or believe) something is going to happen, we tend to act in fairly predictable ways. If we think it's going to rain outside, we'll take an umbrella.

A child who has reached Stage 2 can often figure out what's on somebody's mind, and if he does, he also has a good idea what the person will do. This knowledge will help him know how to act.

A child who has reached Stage 2 has learned these ideas (usually in this order):

> Different people think different things.
> People act based on what they think is going to happen.
> When people think something good will happen, they feel happy (even if it doesn't happen later).
> When people think something bad will happen, they feel unhappy (even if it doesn't happen later).

Do you think Ty (on the left) has reached Stage 2?

Gabe thinks he scored, but it was after the whistle.

It doesn't count.

Ty is certain that Gabe thinks he scored a goal. He makes sure that Gabe knows that the goal doesn't count. He's reached a Stage 2 level of thinking.

Stage 3: Understanding that seeing leads to knowing

At this stage, your child has the ability to understand that a person can know something if he sees it happen for himself. If your child doesn't understand this concept, he'll think you (and other people) see the same things he does, even if it's physically impossible for you to do so.

A child who has reached Stage 3 understands these ideas:

> Just because he sees something doesn't mean that you can see the same thing.
> If he sees something that you can't see, he may need to give you extra verbal information so you can understand.
> If he sees something that you can't see, he may need to give you extra visual information. (For example, he could show, point or turn you toward it so you can see it, too.)

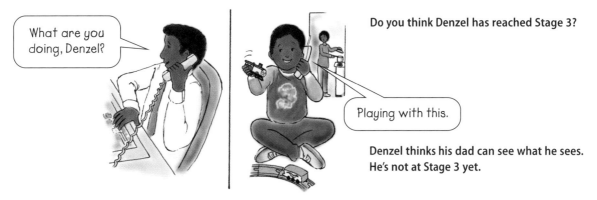

Do you think Denzel has reached Stage 3?

Denzel thinks his dad can see what he sees. He's not at Stage 3 yet.

Stage 4: Understanding hidden feelings

At this stage, your child understands that what we say or how we look isn't always the way we feel inside. If your child understands this, he'll get the point of jokes and will know when someone's teasing, lying or using sarcasm.

At Stage 4, a child understands these ideas:

> People don't always feel the way they appear to.
> People don't always feel the way they say they do.
> Sometimes people hide what they really feel (to tease, to lie or to express humour).

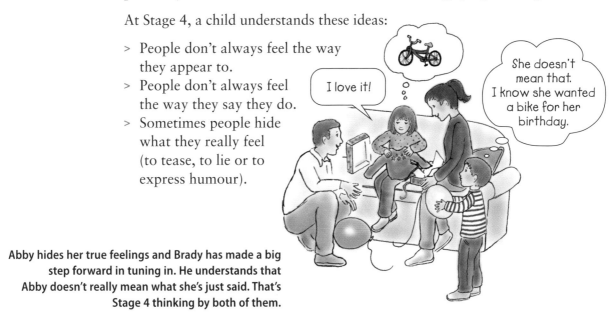

Abby hides her true feelings and Brady has made a big step forward in tuning in. He understands that Abby doesn't really mean what she's just said. That's Stage 4 thinking by both of them.

Stage 5: Understanding false beliefs

At this stage, your child understands that people can sometimes think things are true when they're not. In other words, people sometimes have "false beliefs." Your child understands that he, too, can have a "false belief," and that sometimes a situation turns out differently than he expects. For example, he might think there are cookies in the cookie jar when really there are pennies inside.

Understanding make-believe, such as pretending that a block could be a car or an empty glass is filled with juice, is the first way your child realizes that you can change reality with your imagination.

Later on we realize that people make their decisions based, not on what is true, but on what they think is true.

At Stage 5, a child understands these ideas:

> Sometimes what people believe to be true is not true.
> People act according to what they believe to be true, not what is really true.
> When a person is trying to find something, he looks where he believes the object is, even if that's not where it really is.

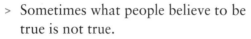
Do you think Ethan is at Stage 5?

Yes!

We'll keep Mom's present in the drawer until tomorrow. Do you think Mom will know her birthday present is in there?

Ethan thinks that because he knows where his mother's present is hidden, she knows it, too. It takes a long time to reach Stage 5.

Talk So Your Child Will Learn to Tune In

As you can see, tuning in is complicated. The good news, though, is that your child can get better at tuning in just by talking and playing with others, especially you.

The best way for him to learn to understand others is to hear you talk about what's going on in other people's minds. That means you should talk often about what you think people are thinking or feeling, and why they're thinking or feeling that way. You should also point out differences of opinion when they occur. ("Your dad thinks it's too hot in here, but I think it's too cold.")

In the next section of this chapter, you'll find lists of words you can use when you talk about what's going on in the minds of others. As you continue to read, you'll find out how to work these words into your conversations with your child.

Eventually, your child might start to use some tuning-in words in his own conversation. Then, equipped with the right language, he can talk about what he's thinking or what someone else is thinking.

By observing, waiting and listening to your child, you can link your tuning-in comments to the things and situations he's interested in. While it's important to include your child's interests, your new ideas don't need to be in response to something he has just said. Nor does your child always have to say something after you do. Of course, he'll learn more about himself and others if he joins in the conversation.

Move your child through the tuning-in stages

Read on to find out the kind of information you can add to help your child progress through the tuning-in stages. Remember, however, that he needs to be a part of the conversation, too (you'll find more on how to involve him in the conversation on page 87).

Emphasize different points of view

Whatever your child's current stage, to become better at tuning in, he must first understand that there's often more than one way to look at a situation. In other words, he needs to know that different people have different opinions about many things.

You can make these different points of view stand out by using contrast words (see list below). For example, "You like chocolate, *but* I *don't* like chocolate. I like vanilla. We like *different* flavours." And "You like green apples, *but* your brother likes the red ones." As you read about each tuning-in stage, you'll find other examples of how to highlight different points of view.

> **Contrast Words**
>
> Same/different
>
> *Positive/negative words (for example,* likes/doesn't like)
>
> All/some
>
> Or
>
> Before/now
>
> Now/later
>
> But
>
> Really

Whenever you use a situation to introduce a new stage of tuning in to your child, start simply. That means begin with comments about what your child wants and thinks. After all, he has to understand himself before he can understand others.

Help your child reach Stage 1 (understanding wanting)

If you're helping your child move into Stage 1, you'll need to help him understand that, in most situations, not everyone wants the same thing he does. Begin by talking about each person's preference. For example: "You want pancakes. Daddy wants a bagel. Briana wants cereal. And I want everyone to be quiet."

When you feel that your child is starting to understand that not everyone always shares his preferences, make some predictions about how someone will feel when they get or don't get what they want. ("Uh-oh, there's no cereal left. Briana is going to be sad.") Then add information about how you or your child can react to that person. ("We can tell her to try the pancakes today.")

> You **like** all of the train books.
> Emma **likes** books with girls in them.
> You and Emma **like** different kinds of books.

Mom uses a trip to the library to talk about the children's different tastes in books.

Below you'll find a list of "want" words that you can use in your conversations to help your child reach Stage 1.

Stage 1: "Want" Words	
Want	Hope
Fancy (UK)	Wish
Like	Dream
Love	Prefer

Stage 1

Move on to Stage 2 (understanding thinking)

If you're trying to get your child to Stage 2, you need to help him think about what others are thinking. Start by including "think" words (see list on the next page) in your conversation in a casual way. The first words to use are "think," "know" and "forget." For example, you can say things like, "Let me think about that," "I think that will be fun," "I know you can do it," "I forgot where my keys are" or "I think it's hot."

This game teaches Alex that there's more than one way to think about what a cloud looks like.

Stage 2: "Think" Words		
Think/Don't think	Believe	Figure out
Know	Expect	Remind
Forget	Feel	Bet
Remember	Imagine	Surprised
Understand	"Have an idea"	Afraid that
Wonder	Guess	

Talking about thinking is one of the best ways for your child to tune in to what's on the minds of others. So build on your child's earliest attempts to talk about what's on his mind.

Young children use some "think" words more to keep the conversation going than to talk about thinking. For example, your child might say, "Know what?" or "Remember when we saw the giraffe?" just to start a conversation. He might answer your questions with "I think so" when he means "yes." You might hear "I don't know" a lot from your child. That sentence probably means your child either can't answer your question or doesn't feel like answering.

When your child uses a "think" word in this way, act as if he's really trying to talk about what he's thinking. On the following page, look at how Ben's mother interprets his "I don't know" answer.

Mom treats Ben's "I don't know" as if it were a real "think" statement. She "thinks aloud" about what might have happened.

Understanding a specific kind of grammar can help your child tune in to what's going on in someone else's mind. Consider sentences like these: "He thinks that the fish are hungry," "He knows how to do it," "He remembers when my birthday is." This kind of sentence—beginning with a "think" word and followed by words such as "that" or "how"—tells your child that you're talking about someone else's point of view. He needs to hear this kind of grammar so he can use it in his own speech. Sometimes you might leave out the "that": "He says (that) he likes you." Your child will need to hear you use complicated language like this many times before he can begin to understand and use it himself.

Study the list of "think" words on page 77. Make sure you use a variety of them, but concentrate at first on "think," "know" and "forget." This will help your child understand that there are different ways to talk about thinking.

When your child starts to tune in to the thoughts of others, don't get stuck just listing what people want or think. Help your child understand why people think the way they do so he can make some predictions about people's behaviour. Use linking words like those shown in the list below to explain why others feel the way they do.

Linking words

Because	Before/after
If...then	So
When (*When something is done, the result is...*)	
After (*After something is done, the result is...*)	

Linking Words

Use sentences like these when you talk to your child: "Annie's sad *because* she wanted the bicycle," "*If* I give Jon a piece of cake, *then* he'll be happy," "*When* he wants something, he'll ask for it over and over," "*After* I give him my train, he'll like me" or "He doesn't like swimming, *so* he's staying home."

Move on to Stage 3 (understanding that seeing leads to knowing)

If you're working on moving your child into Stage 3, let him know that you don't see what he sees. Whenever he incorrectly assumes you have the same information as him, just say something like, "I can't see it. Show me so I can see what you're seeing" or "Tell me what it is, so I know what you're looking at."

Be a good model for your child by turning a book you're sharing directly toward him at times, explaining what you're doing and why ("Here, I'll turn the book so you can see the picture"). Try pointing out something that you notice and he doesn't ("Look at that red bird. Do you see it?") and maybe he'll do the same for you.

> **Stage 3: "See" Words**
>
> | | |
> |---|---|
> | Sees | Show |
> | Doesn't see | Look |
> | Tell (*about what's not seen*) | |

Reminding Denzel that Dad can't see the train, Mom suggests that Denzel tell Dad what he's doing.

Move on to Stage 4 (understanding hidden feelings)

Eventually, your child must realize that people sometimes hide their feelings and say things that are different from what they really think. To progress into Stage 4, your child needs to focus on what people say and then consider what they may be thinking but not expressing in words.

Look over the list of "hidden feeling" words on the next page and, when you're with your child, try using them in ways that reveal what the people around him aren't saying directly to him. You'll notice that many of the words in the list are communication words ("say," "ask," "tell," "whisper," "tease" and "promise") that are used when we want to quote other people. So when you're ready to begin using this vocabulary with your child, start by getting him used to hearing you quote what you've heard others say ("Daddy *says* it's cold outside today").

The next step is highlighting the difference between what people say or do and how they really feel by using "hidden feeling" words in combination with some of the contrast words that you learned earlier in this chapter. Try saying to your child something like, "He *says* he's not going to eat the cookies, *but* I don't think he *means* it." Other contrast words that are particularly useful at this stage are "really" ("He's telling me he's not hungry, but *really* he wants a cookie") and positive/negative combinations ("He says he *doesn't* want another cookie; I think he *does* want one").

Mom uses the words "say" and "but" to make sure Mike understands that what his brother says and what is really true are two different things.

Next, set the stage for your child to use the "hidden feeling" words himself. For instance, ask him, "What does that sneaky smile on his face mean?" Ideally, he'll answer you with a statement like, "He says he won't eat the cookies, but he will."

Your child might enjoy hearing what his stuffed animals or puppets have to say, especially if it's something silly and different from what's real. For instance, if Cookie Monster says, "Me eat cookies and little boys too," you could explain, "Cookie Monster says that he eats little boys, but he doesn't. He only eats cookies." And let a big smile on your face show him you're joking.

> ### Stage 4: "Hidden Feeling" Words
>
> *These words can all be used to talk about the difference between what people say and what they really mean.*
>
> | | | | |
> |---|---|---|---|
> | Say | Ask | Really | Mean *(as in "He means what he says")* |
> | Whisper | Tease | Promise | |
> | Tell | Truth/lie | Joke | |

Aunt Rhoda **says** that she's coming to see you later. Here... she wants to talk to you.

Mom tells Emily what Aunt Rhoda said and then lets Emily hear for herself.

Just like "think" words, "hidden feeling" words are often followed by "that," "about" and "what," as in "He said that he liked you" (or just "He said he liked you"), "He told me about his dog" and "She asked what the story was about."

Figuring out how someone really feels can be hard even for the most sensitive person. Often the best clues to what's really going on inside people's heads can be found in their body language, tone of voice and facial expression. Point these clues out to your child as they appear. ("She says she likes the sweater. But I don't think she means it. She sounds sad, and she's not smiling.")

A fun way for your child to learn about hidden meanings is through jokes and puns. You'll probably have to start with an explanation about why the punch line is funny. For example, you say, "Knock, knock." Your child says, "Who's there?" You say, "Luke." Your child says, "Luke who?" You say, "Luke behind you! Oh, there's no one there." Then if you need to, add an explanation: "That's funny because Luke is a boy's name, but I meant 'look.' 'Luke' and 'look' sound the same, but they're not." If your child has trouble getting the joke, try showing him pictures of a boy (Luke) and a pair of eyes (look).

Move on to Stage 5 (understanding false beliefs)

You've already started to help your child understand false beliefs by talking about what people think, believe and know. That's because what goes on in someone's mind (for example, what the person remembers or expects to happen) is so often different from real life. As your child approaches Stage 5, you need to point those differences out to him as they arise.

> The older boy **thought** the monster was mean because of the way he looks. But his younger brother knew better – **really**, he was nice.

Mom wants Max to understand that the children in the story had two different opinions about the monster, and only one of them was really true.

Helping your child understand that people's actions are based on what they think is true (even though it might not be true) can actually be fun. Family life presents lots of opportunities for playing tricks on people. It will be easier for your child to understand a false-belief situation if you talk to him about the trick ahead of time ("Let's fool Daddy") and then let him participate in setting the trick up. Look at how Ethan's dad in the pictures on the next page involves him in hiding Mom's birthday present.

If you use specific words (like those listed below) to explain what the other person is probably thinking (for example, "Mom thinks we don't have a present") and what's really going on ("but we *really* do have one"), your child will gradually realize that not everyone is always in on the joke.

Stage 5: "False Belief" Words

Real/pretend	Know
Trick	Remember
Fool	Expect
Think	

Stage 5

In helping your child tune in to others, you will be constantly looking at two sides of every story, focusing on the different opinions people have. Knowing that there are two ways of looking at something helps your child solve problems. It gives him choices in difficult moments. For example, if your children are fighting over where to sit in the car, you could say, "You can sit in the front seat *some* of the time, *but* not *all* of the time," or "Do you want to sit in the front seat *now* or *later?*"

Look at how Christopher's mother talks to him when he and his sister fight over the same toy.

You can play with the pony **now** or **later.**

Later is in 15 minutes.

When's later?

Words that give your child a choice come in handy for solving problems.

Highlight what you say

In Chapter 2, you read how the Four S's can make your actions, gestures and facial expressions easier for your child to understand. Using the Four S's when you talk to your child about tuning in will make the key words stand out and be more meaningful.

Say less

Even if your child speaks in long, complicated sentences, he might not understand yours. Make your sentences easy to understand by using words he's very familiar with. Keep the sentences short and the grammar simple.

Sentences that comment on what someone else thinks or says—for example, "He thinks that the fish are hungry"—can be hard for your child to understand. If he doesn't understand them, break the more complex sentence down into two simple ones and then build them up into one again, like this: "He's thinking about the fish. The fish might be hungry. He thinks that the fish are hungry."

Always talk naturally. Saying less doesn't mean leaving out words like "a" and "the."

Stress

Make the tuning-in words stand out. Vary your voice by saying these words more loudly or quietly. Match your tone of voice to the feeling and thoughts you're talking about. In the picture below, Brady's father exaggerates all the words that will help him understand why his sister might not be happy with her present.

Dad stresses the tuning-in words.

Your child might not grasp these abstract ideas at first. So make sure you find many similar situations to stress the key tuning-in words. For example, Brady's dad could show disappointment when he doesn't get what he wants at dinnertime. "I *really* wanted pasta, but I'll tell Mom I'm happy with chicken."

Go Slow

Your child needs time to understand new ideas and new language, so slow down when you're introducing them. Say the key words very slowly and distinctly. You can also try pausing after you say a tuning-in word to draw his attention to it.

Remember to wait long enough after you say something to give him time to respond. Always speak naturally, making sure you keep the rhythms and sounds of normal speech.

Show

Remember from Chapter 2 that there are a few ways to show your child what you're talking about. You can show him by pointing; by adding actions, gestures and facial expressions; or by using pictures.

Show or point to the person or thing you're talking about

Simply by pointing to another person, you can help your child understand whose point of view you're talking about. This will help when you're trying to highlight the differences between your child and others. Pointing can also help your child understand who said or thought something.

You **like** all of the train books. *Emma* **likes** books with girls in them. *You* and *Emma* **like different** kinds of books.

Mom points to Luc to emphasize how his reading tastes differ from Emma's.

Show with actions, gestures and facial expressions

Adding actions, gestures and facial expressions will help your child understand what you're saying. For example, if you're thinking something out, narrow your eyes and put your fist under your chin (in thinking position). If you're talking about something you don't believe to be true, show your disbelief with your mouth open wide and hands on hips.

Show with pictures and writing

Especially if your child is a visual learner, you can use paper and pen to help him understand some complex ideas and grammar. For example, try explaining the differences between what people say and think by drawing cartoon-style talk and thought bubbles like these:

Write what someone thinks inside a thought bubble.

Write what someone says inside a talk bubble.

Simple drawings (you don't have to be an artist!) can help your child understand what someone else is thinking. For instance, if you see him watching fish swimming near the top of the water, you could show him the picture on the left and say, "You think the fish are hungry."

You can also draw a picture to help explain to your child what someone could do or say, based on what the person is thinking. For instance, if he agrees that he thinks the fish are hungry, you could use this picture to suggest what he could say.

(Chapter 13 will give you more details about using talk and thought bubbles.)

Help Your Child Talk About Tuning In

When your child has got used to hearing you use tuning-in words, you can encourage him to start using them, too. With the right words and grammar, he'll be able to talk about what's on his mind and other people's minds. In a back-and-forth conversation with you, he can also start deciding how his actions might make others feel.

To get your child involved in a tuned-in conversation, remember your I-Cues.

The I's...	The Cues...
> Include	> **Comment**... and wait
> Interpret	> **Ask a question**... and wait
> Introduce	> **Make it easier to answer your question**... and wait
> Insist	> **Hint**... and wait
	> **Make a suggestion**... and wait
	> **Tell your child what to say or do**... and wait

Your questions will probably get him talking the most. The trick is not to ask question after question. That will probably make him stop talking!

Ask open-ended questions that encourage your child to stretch his thinking skills: "Why is Annie sad?" "What can you do to make her feel better?" "What did Little Red Riding Hood say to Grandma?" Remember that these are difficult questions. So if your child can't answer, try easier ones: "Is Annie sad?" "What did she want for her birthday?" "What did she get?" Give helpful hints and wait for your child to come to his own conclusions. For example, it might be too hard for your child to answer a question like, "Why do you think she's unhappy with her present?" Instead, you can ask an easier question, maybe a fill-in-the-blank one, such as, "She wanted a bike and she got a...?" Or, as a last resort, take your child's turn and answer the question yourself.

You might be surprised by how many opportunities there are for you and your child to talk about thinking and feeling. Look at how many tuning-in words James and his mother use as they plan where to get his jacket. Notice how she balances her questions with a similar number of comments to involve him in their discussion.

Mother: Where do you *think* (that) we should go to get a jacket?

James: From the jacket place.

Mother: A clothing store, you *mean*?

James: Do you *think* they have a jacket at Lowry's?

Mother: We could check at Lowry's. There are two of them. Which one do you *mean*?

James: *Remember* Lowry's on Jarvis Street? Do you *think* they have a jacket?

Mother: You *know* what? When we were there the other day, I didn't see any jackets. That's a small store. The bigger store might have them.

James: I *think* so.

Play tuning in games

Many simple games provide opportunities to get your child to think and wonder and talk about tuning in. You can play some of these games anytime and anywhere, even making them up yourself. For example, if your child picks out his favourite T-shirt to wear, let him know that you like it, too. Then take turns talking about which clothes you both like. In the grocery store, take turns listing what you like and don't like as you fill up the cart together.

Try playing guessing games. Guess what the clouds look like. Look at abstract art—or let your child make his own masterpiece—and talk about what you both see ("I *think* it's an old man"). Talk about which animals resemble people you know ("The owl *reminds* me of Grandpa"). Or guess what's for dinner ("I *wonder* what Dad is making for dinner tonight").

Hiding games such as "Watch My Eyes and Find a Surprise" (described on page 32) are good for helping your child learn that "seeing leads to knowing." Below you can read about how to play another kind of hiding game. It will encourage your child to understand that he has to give extra information when someone else can't see what he sees.

The Barrier Game

> Set up a screen or a barrier on a table so that your child can't see what you will put behind it.

> Have your child close his eyes. Then put an object behind the screen so that you can see it, but he can't.

> Give your child bits of information about the unseen object (for example, "It's a fruit" or "It's red") and let him guess what it is.

> Then give your child a turn at hiding something behind the barrier and giving you information.

Another fun game that helps your child talk about what others say is "Broken Telephone." This game works best with three or more people, but you can also play with just the two of you. Each person takes a turn whispering a word or sentence in the other person's ear. The last person must report what he heard by saying, "He said..." (or "She said...") and repeating the words that were whispered into his (or her) ear.

Games make talking about tuning in fun.

Tuning-in skills take time to develop. No one expects your child to understand all the complicated workings of other people's thoughts. After all, even as adults, most of us can never quite figure out why others do certain things. But with practice, the right kind of support from you and plenty of time, your child's "mind reading" skills will grow, changing forever the way he thinks about others.

Learn About the World Together

6

By tuning in better, your child may be starting to understand how other people think and feel. But there are still so many important things your child needs to learn about the world. Think of all the questions he could ask you. There are the easy ones, like, "What's for dinner?" or "What flavour is your ice cream?" And then there are the harder ones, like, "Where do birds go in winter?" "What does 'hanging out' mean?" and "Why are there lines on Grandma's face?"

While you might not have the answers to every question, to your child you are the expert. That doesn't mean he expects you to know everything. It's actually more fun for him if you and he can search for the answers together.

Your child already knows that by talking and listening to you he can gather basic information about his life, such as what's on the menu for dinner or when it's bath-time. This chapter will show you how, with your help, he can start using conversation to explore the world.

Add New Ideas

When you talk with your child, your comments about his interests should extend or stretch his thinking. Some of the things you say will be facts ("Dinosaurs lived millions of years ago"). Factual information adds to your child's knowledge.

Other things you say to your child should be more abstract. When you talk about things like the past or the future, for instance, he'll have to visualize what you're saying entirely in his mind. Because it goes beyond the here and now, abstract information makes children think a little harder.

Your child needs both kinds of information to learn about the world, so whenever you talk with your child, try to add new ideas. That means build on his interests with comments that will make him think differently about something. Your child has already learned to talk. Now it's time for him to talk to learn. Keep reading for tips to get the most out of this strategy.

Help Your Child Join the Conversation

If you involve your child in the discussion, he'll have a chance to add some new ideas of his own. So remind yourself to pause or wait every time you make a comment or ask a question, to give your child a chance to talk.

If commenting (and waiting) isn't enough to encourage him to take his turn, try the other Cues (questions, hints, suggestions, visual cues) you read about in Chapter 4. And don't forget to use the Four S's to make it easier for him to understand you.

Talk about the past

By reminiscing with you about family events, such as a camping trip or a visit to the zoo, your child gets his first experiences in talking about the past. As you share memories of weeks ago or even earlier the same day, he discovers the joy of talking about his life with someone else. Remembering happy (and even not-so-happy) times spent with his family also gives him a sense of belonging.

Families vary in how often they talk about the past. If your child frequently hears family members discussing past events, he's more likely to want to talk about the past himself.

If your child gets lots of practice talking about the past with you, eventually he might also want to share his stories with others. (You'll find out how to help him become a story-teller in Chapter 8.)

Make memories with your child

It will be easier to talk about the past with your child when the event you're talking about is something the two of you have done together. That's why your early conversations about the past will often be about highlights of the day or memorable moments from a special event, like a birthday celebration.

When you're with your child on one of these occasions—it could be just a trip to a grocery store or an afternoon of playing at a park—you can highlight all the events and feelings that are important for him to remember later on. Look at how one mother highlights her son's visit to a farm, as it's happening; later on, she prompts him to remember all the highlights:

The babies are drinking **milk** from the mommy pig.

They're very hungry...Let's hurry so we can see the **goats!** I wish we had **more time.**

Those pigs are hungry.

Mom stresses some things that Colin can talk about later.

Colin, tell Dad about the baby pigs we saw at the farm.

What animals did we see after the pigs?

They were getting **milk** from their mommy.

The **goats.** But we needed **more time.**

Back at home, Mom guides Colin's memories with some questions and comments. Since Mom made the key events and feelings stand out earlier, Colin has no trouble remembering them now.

Use visual cues to help you and your child remember

You aren't always with your child. He goes to school, for instance, and he probably visits friends without you. Making conversation about something your child did when you weren't there can be challenging. Here's one solution: ask the people who have been with your child during the day to fill you in through pictures and written messages.

For example, to bridge the gap between home and school, ask your child's teacher to send home some written notes about what happened that day. She might also send other mementos from the day: your child's art work, stones from the playground  or classroom toys. These objects will remind him to tell you something about his day. And if he doesn't initiate conversation about them on his own, the mementos will give you something to go on.

Even when you have been with your child, the two of you might forget some of the things you've done on a busy day. So take home souvenirs from your outings. Something like a menu, a bus ticket or a photograph might help jog your child's memories.

Make links to the past

Another way to talk about the past is to link current experiences with things that have happened to your child in the past. For example, if the two of you see a group of children playing soccer, and your child once played the game, you could say: "Look, they're playing soccer. You played soccer last year." Or, if a picture of a sandcastle in a book reminds you of one you and your child made together, you might say, "We made a sandcastle like that one when we went to the beach."

When you make this kind of connection, you show your child that the past is a real part of who we are and what's going on around us. Introducing him to the idea that there's more than one way (his own) of experiencing things is a valuable lesson in itself.

These pictures are from your first birthday party. Look how little you were. Daddy had a lot more hair then!

Talking about how he and his father looked in the past is a good way for Jose to understand that there are different ways of seeing the same people.

Use time words

There are certain time words and phrases that will help your child understand that you're talking about the past, such as "last night," "yesterday" and "then and now" ("Then you were little; now you are big"). Naming the day that you're talking about will help ("On Sunday, we played games"). And so will using action words in the past tense ("He talked to me," "He played with me" and "I ran").

There are also words that let you order the events of the past—for example, "then" (as in "Then we ate"), "next" ("Next we went outside"), "before/after" ("We swam before we ate") and "first/last" ("We ate the red ones last"). So stress these words and use them over and over in your conversations with your child.

Talk about past feelings

Finally, use the past to discuss how your child and others felt about what happened. For example, if you're reminiscing about a trip to a high bridge, you might say something like this: "Remember how scared your sister was to walk on that bridge? You weren't scared at all." It's easier to think about emotions when you and your child have some distance from the events that caused the feelings.

> Most young children learn to talk about one day's events in the right order before they recall the order of events that were weeks or months apart. That kind of talk about the past comes a few years later.

(Chapter 8 will give you more information on how to work stories about past events into your conversations with your child.)

Talk about the future

Conversations about the future are harder for your child to understand simply because the future hasn't happened yet. You're talking about what "might possibly" or "could" happen. Understanding what he can't see requires him to take a leap of the imagination.

The only way that your child will develop an understanding of future time is by hearing you talk about what's going to happen. The following suggestions will guide you when you talk about the future with your child:

> Talk about the future during daily routines.
> Talk about familiar future events.
> Plan future events together.
> Problem-solve for the future.
> Use time words.
> Use visual cues.

Talk about the future during daily routines

One of the first times your child will hear you talk about the future will be during his daily routines, such as bath-time, bedtime, meals and getting dressed.

For example, think about what you might have said when your child learned the steps involved in brushing his teeth: "First, you're going to take the top off the toothpaste... And then you're going to put the toothpaste on the toothbrush... Next, you're going to brush your teeth... And then you're going to rinse your mouth." As your child learns to brush his teeth, he begins to anticipate what's going to happen next in the routine.

So, if your child is just starting to think and talk about the future, use daily routines to get him used to it. You can encourage him to think about the next step by asking questions and stressing certain words that let him know you're talking about the future. For example, "And *then* what?" and "What happens *next?*" and "What are you *going* to do?"

Talk about familiar future events

Once your child has had lots of practice talking about the future during daily routines, try having similar conversations about familiar future events. These are events that your child can imagine easily because they've happened before. For example, you could talk with him about a return visit to a friend's house or the doctor's office, a vacation or a birthday party.

To get your child to predict what might happen, start with what he's already experienced and remembers well. Then use the past as a springboard for talking about the future. See how Harry's mother does that in the illustration shown on the next page.

Harry's mother uses his memory of his last vacation to plan the next one with him.

Plan future events together

Most of the time, the future is not completely predictable. There are many words that suggest something is possible or uncertain. "Might," "maybe," "perhaps," "possibly," "probably," "could," "not sure" and "guess" are a few. Sentences like, "We might go the park" or "If it rains, the game could be cancelled" show your child that the future isn't always certain.

One way to introduce your child to this idea—and to the words that express it—is to plan future events together. Involving your child in plans for what's coming up helps him learn that he has some control over his life.

Start by talking about what "might" or "could" happen. Then give your child a chance to plan for how it might turn out by asking him his opinion. In the illustration below, Ben's dad shows how easy this can be.

By asking Ben if he would like to go skiing, Dad gives Ben a role in deciding what will happen the next day.

Problem-solve for the future

Talking about the future also involves thinking about problems that might come up and planning what to do about them. Some potential problems and their solutions will be about non-emotional events, as in this bath-time observation: "If we put too much water in the tub, it will spill over onto the floor when you get in. So let's turn the water off when the tub is just half-full."

Other problem-solving situations ask your child to predict how someone will feel based on something that has happened or will happen. Look what happens when Brady realizes how Abby will feel when she doesn't get the present she wants.

Brady predicts how Abby will feel because he knows that she's not going to be happy with her present. And Dad finds a solution to the problem.

(In Chapter 13 you'll read more about solving problems and taking other people's feelings into consideration.)

Use time words

Your child might not know how the calendar works yet (children usually learn this between ages six and eight). But by talking about the future with you, he can begin to understand that something will happen "soon" or is still "a long time away."

To make sure Eric understands what "soon" means, Mom gives him some extra information.

Use the words "then" and "next" to order events in the future, too: "We're going to see the stop sign, and *then* we'll turn down the winding road. *Next* thing you know, we'll be at Grandma's house."

Use visual cues

Some children find it easier to understand and talk about the future if they see a picture of what's going to happen. You can show just one picture, as Jackson's mother does in the picture below. Or you might find a written list or a picture schedule to be a useful way of getting your child to discuss the things that could possibly happen.

It's easier for Jackson to imagine the TV his family is going to buy when he sees a picture of it.

You could use a "First/Then" board like this to talk about the idea that your child needs to do his homework before he plays on the computer.

Add details

Your child probably likes learning specific details about people, things or situations that he's interested in. If he's a train buff, he could be open to hearing about different kinds of trains or people who work on trains. If he's a big music fan, he may happily listen to any detail about Mozart or Madonna. So when you're sharing interesting facts with him, try stretching his mind a little by describing something in a new way.

The comments you add to the conversation present golden opportunities to introduce your child to new words. Of course, when you do, take a moment to explain the meaning carefully.

When Mom explains what "nocturnal" means, Ben not only understands the word but uses it himself.

Tell a little...then tell a little bit more

Sometimes your comments might be more abstract, to help your child think about things that he hasn't experienced. How complicated your descriptions are depends on your child's level of understanding. So if your child is just starting to be interested in getting information, begin simply by adding one detail at a time.

For example, to describe a fish that your child sees in a tank, you could just say its name: "That fish is called a salmon." If, however, your child wants to know more, you could add something like this: "Salmon live in the ocean. When they're ready to have babies, they swim all the way back to the river where they were born."

Make comparisons

Your descriptions could also compare one thing to another. For example, you could say, "Wool is much warmer than cotton" or "Oranges are sweeter than grapefruit." Try to use the contrast words we talked about in Chapter 5 (see page 75) to describe things: "Micky's guitar is loud, *but* your drums are *really* loud."

If you talk this way about familiar things, your child will get plenty of practice with the kind of language he needs to talk about people's different points of view. For instance, he'll be able to say: "Gabe thinks he's the best player, but he's wrong. I'm the best."

Talk about imagining and pretending

Imagining and pretending make your child think of the world in an entirely different way. Pretend play is so important to your child's learning that this book has a whole chapter about it (see Chapter 9). In the meantime, introduce your child to the word "pretend" and the special way children talk when they pretend by using the key phrase "pretend that" (or just "pretend" without "that"). For instance, you could suggest, "Let's pretend that we're puppies" (or "Let's pretend we're puppies").

I have a little bird in *my* hand.

It's not a real bird. It's a **pretend** bird.

Let me see.

Dad makes the word "pretend" stand out so Brady understands that he's holding an imaginary bird.

Let's **pretend** that it's flying south for the winter.

Let's **pretend** that he's flying to Florida!

Next, Dad adds a new idea about what the imaginary bird is doing.

Give explanations

In Chapter 5 we talked about giving your child explanations for how people feel when they want things, such as, "Annie's sad because she wanted a bicycle (not a sweater) for her birthday." But more factual explanations—"We can't go swimming because it's raining"—are useful, too. They'll help your child become familiar with the words that introduce explanations, such as "because," "so," "if/then," "when" (as in "When the rooster crows, it's time for the other animals to wake up") or "that means" (as in "That means she wants her bottle").

Look for opportunities to give your child reasons for what is happening— "Daddy put out bread crumbs so that the birds will have dinner," for instance, or "If you don't wear your jacket, then you'll be cold at the park."

Talk about feelings and thoughts

As you've read before, talking about what causes someone to feel a certain way can make your child consider someone else's point of view. But you don't have to always talk about the causes. Just pointing out how others are feeling or getting your child's opinion on his own emotions or someone else's will help him become more tuned in.

In family life there are many opportunities to talk about feelings.

It's probably not a surprise that research shows that mothers tend to talk more about their feelings than fathers. That means some fathers may have to work a little harder at using this kind of language.

You don't want to overwhelm your child with too many ideas at once. Just make one or two interesting comments and then wait for him to add his own. As you've read in this chapter and in Chapter 5, there are lots of choices for what to say. Look at all the ideas you can add when you talk to your child about dinosaurs:

TALK ABOUT TUNING IN TO OTHERS
"I think all the plant-eating dinosaurs were afraid of the meat-eating dinosaurs."

TALK ABOUT THE PAST
"Dinosaurs lived millions of years ago."

Make links to the past
"We saw a dinosaur just like that in your video."

TALK ABOUT THE FUTURE
"Maybe we'll see dinosaurs at the museum tomorrow."

GIVE EXPLANATIONS
"Maybe dinosaurs disappeared because they couldn't find food any more."

ADD DETAILS
"This dinosaur is called a stegosaurus. It ate plants."

TALK ABOUT FEELINGS AND THOUGHTS
"You get mad when your brother plays with your dinosaurs."

TALK ABOUT IMAGINING AND PRETENDING
"Imagine that dinosaurs were living in our backyard."

There may have been a time when your goal was for your child to learn to talk. This chapter is a reminder that once he's talking, there's still a lot more for him to discover. At this point in your child's development, it's not about learning to talk; it's about talking to learn.

7

Stay Tuned In with Books

Books are a great way to tune in to others. Reading books to children introduces them to situations and lives that are different from their own— and to new ways of looking at the world.

The best way to help your child tune in through a book is for the two of you to talk about it as you read together. For instance, you can talk about what the characters want, how they think and feel, and why they're acting the way they are.

In this chapter we'll look at how you can sharpen your child's tuning-in skills while the two of you share the wonders to be found in books. Your simple conversations with him during reading sessions will open his mind to new ideas and adventures.

What to Read

In today's bookstores and libraries, there is no shortage of books to interest any child. The problem parents usually face when selecting children's books isn't finding suitable, high-quality books but choosing from among hundreds of them.

Children's books come in two basic kinds. Fiction books tell imaginary stories about people or non-human characters (such as animals) that act and feel like people. Non-fiction books for children present information about real people or things, such as trains or the stars. Both kinds of book give your child valuable learning experiences.

When it's time to work on your child's tuning-in skills, however, pick either fiction books or non fiction ones with interesting stories about people. Also look for these types of books:

> Books that he shows an interest in
> Books with simple plots—stories with a clear beginning, middle and end
> Books about unfamiliar situations—such as life on a farm or in a foreign country (to get his imagination working and start him thinking about different points of view)
> Books where the pictures don't always match the text—so you can discuss things that aren't mentioned in the story ("Why do you think he's smiling in that picture?")
> Books without any words—so he can make up the story on his own just by looking at the pictures
> Books where the main character has to solve a problem
> Homemade books—scrapbooks with souvenirs from places your child has been and photo albums of special events, to help him talk about the past
> Books that target a specific communication goal—For example, a book that asks and answers questions can help your child learn this kind of grammar. And a book with dialogue (such as "He said, 'You're late!'") will give your child models for quoting what other people say. Remember that when your child can talk about what someone else says, he's starting to tune in to that person's thinking.

Little Red Riding Hood said, "Your voice sounds funny, Grandma!" Then, what did "Grandma" say to Little Red Riding Hood?

She said, "I have a cold!"

Books with dialogue give your child a chance to try out other people's words and realize that people don't always tell the truth.

A Very Short List of Recommended Books

Understanding different points of view (see page 70)

Look for books that present characters who hold different points of view or problems that can be solved in more than one way.

***Good Night, Gorilla* by Peggy Rathmann**
The zookeeper doesn't realize that the gorilla is letting all the animals out of their cages.

***King Bidgood's in the Bathtub* by Audrey Wood and Don Wood**
When the king refuses to come out of the bathtub, his subjects try to solve the problem.

***Seven Blind Mice* by Ed Young**
Seven blind mice try to guess what the strange creature at the pond really is.

Understanding wanting (see page 71)

Look for books where characters have dreams and desires and stories that describe what they do to get what they want.

***Bread and Jam for Frances* by Russell Hoban and Lillian Hoban**
Frances wants to eat the same thing for every meal.

***When I Get Bigger* by Mercer Mayer**
Little Critter dreams of all the things that he hopes to do when he's older.

Understanding thinking (see page 72)

Look for books that talk about the characters' thoughts.

***There's a Nightmare in My Closet* by Mercer Mayer**
A little boy thinks there's a monster in his closet.

***The Runaway Bunny* by Margaret Wise Brown and Clement Hurd**
A mother rabbit imagines many ways to rescue her young runaway bunny.

Understanding that seeing leads to knowing (see page 73)

Look for books with hidden objects that you and your child can search for together.

***Can You See What I See? Seymour and the Juice Box Boat* by Walter Wick**
From a series of photo books in which children are asked to find specific objects.

Understanding hidden feelings (see page 73)

Look for books where the characters hide their true feelings.

***The Adventures of Pinocchio* by Carlo Collodi**
A puppet's nose grows whenever he tells a lie.

Understanding false beliefs (see page 74)

Look for books where there is some trickery going on.

***Little Red Riding Hood* by the Brothers Grimm**
The wolf tricks Little Red Riding Hood by pretending to be her grandmother.

***The Emperor's New Clothes* by Hans Christian Andersen**
The emperor is tricked into wearing invisible clothes.

How to Read to Your Child

Sometimes the words and the pictures on the page won't be enough to keep your child interested in a book. To keep the story exciting, you'll have to use your voice almost as an actor would. Pointing to the pictures or words should help keep his attention. But also keep in mind that, when you read to your child, part of your job is to have a conversation with him about the book.

To make a good story come alive, you can draw on many of the ideas discussed in earlier chapters of this book. First, get face to face. When the two of you are reading, this means make it easy for your child to look at you and the book. You'll also find that the I-Cues (especially Include your child's interests and Ask a question) come in handy in this situation, as do the Four S's. How these basic ideas relate to book reading is discussed in detail below.

Get face to face for reading

When you read, make sure that your child can see your face when he needs to. Most of the time, he will look at the book. However, you also want him to be able to shift his attention easily from the book to you. Your expressions should tell him as much as your words.

So when you can, get face to face by sitting across from your child, with the book between you. Or, if he's on your lap or beside you, poke your head around during the book's most exciting parts so he can look into your eyes.

Another benefit of being face to face is that you can follow what he's looking at on the page. This will help you focus your conversation on the things in the book that interest him most.

Any time you want your child to notice you, use some of the "hooks" and other ideas described in Chapter 2. Do the unexpected. Make mistakes on purpose. Use fun words and a fun voice. And always remember to pause at key moments.

Use your I's (Include, Interpret, Introduce, Insist)

Begin by including his interests: read books about the things he's interested in. Don't worry if he only wants to read information books, such as ones about dinosaurs or airplanes. There are lots of different ways to talk about something. Even while looking at a train catalogue, you can still insert tuning-in words: "Which train do you like the best?" or "Do you remember when we saw a train like that?"

If your child wants to read only information books, try introducing fiction books about his favourite topics. For example, if he likes to read about dinosaurs, he might enjoy a story about a little boy with a pet dinosaur who gets lost. Eventually your child's interests should expand.

Regardless of what the book is about, your child will have his own ideas about what he finds interesting. Notice what he's looking at in the book and follow up by talking about that specific picture. Include his ideas and words in your conversation to let him know you're listening and show that you value his opinion. If you're not sure what he's saying, interpret what you think he means and check with him to make sure you're right. And then make a comment or two of your own, adding new information and ideas.

If, however, your child only wants to talk about one thing, you'll have to insist on getting the reading (and the conversation) back on track. If you've developed a sign to warn him about talking non-stop (such as holding your hand up, palm toward him, or bringing your index finger to your mouth as if to say "be quiet"), use it. You may even need to give him a firm but friendly warning that you're going to change the topic. After all, he can only learn to think about different points of view if hears them. Remember, too, that the best way to make sure your child lets you take a turn is to focus on what he does right (for example, by saying something like, "Thanks for listening to me").

Ask questions to cue your child to take his turn

Talking about the book should be a back-and-forth conversation between you and your child. Sometimes you can encourage your child to talk about what's happening by making a comment about what's going on in the book and waiting for him to respond. Often, however, you'll need to use questions.

First, ask questions to make sure your child understands the story. Before you begin discussing the feelings and thoughts of the characters in the book, find out if your child understands the plot—who the characters are, what they're doing and why they're doing it.

If you're reading *Little Red Riding Hood*, you might ask, "Can you tell me what the little girl is doing?" If your child answers, "She's putting on her coat," include his words in what you say next and add a comment with your own idea ("Yes, she's putting on her coat. She's going on a long trip."). If you wait long enough, your child might add another piece of information. If he doesn't, you could try an open-ended question that asks him to explain part of the story ("Why did Little Red Riding Hood's mother pack food in the basket?"). If your child can't answer a question like that one, try some closed Wh- questions ("Who is Little Red Riding Hood going to visit?" or "Where is Little Red Riding Hood going?"). These questions require only one- or two-word answers (for example, "Grandma").

When you know your child is following the story, ask more open-ended questions to get him to think along with the character. For example, "What do you think will happen next?" is a good open-ended question that makes your child think about what the character might do. (To review the topic of closed and open questions, see pages 60–61.)

What did the little boy plant?

A seed.

That's right. He planted a seed. He put the seed in the ground and watered it every day. What do you think happened next?

A big carrot growed.

First, Mom asks Matthew a closed Wh- question to make sure that he knows what the story is about. Then she repeats his words to show him that she agrees with his answer and follows up with some information of her own. Finally, she asks a more open-ended question to help him get more involved in the story.

Knowing when to ask questions is an essential part of reading to your child. To make sure he is following the story, ask simple information questions ("Who's that at the door?" "What has he got in his hand?" "Where is she going?") at natural break points in the story, such as the end of a page or a chapter. Ask questions that encourage him to come up with his own opinions and ideas when you're close to the part of the story that you want him to talk about. For example, after you read a scary part of a story, stop right away to ask your child how he would feel in the same situation. You might say something like, "How does that monster make you feel?"

If your child finds interruptions during the story upsetting, you can try saving your questions and comments until the end of the book. Then, next time you read the book, try again to ask one or two easy-to-answer questions at the logical break points, such as the end of the first page. If your child still insists on reading the book without interruptions, find a new book that he's never heard read from beginning to end. Divide your reading sessions between "read only" books and "talk and read" books.

To avoid turning your child off with too many questions, remember to combine your questions ("What's the gorilla doing?") with comments ("That's a pretty smart gorilla!") and hints ("I wonder where all the animals are going"). And if your child says something you don't understand, let him know so he can try to tell you again more clearly.

Tips for asking questions when you read with your child

1. Ask a question…WAIT for an answer
2. Include your child's words…and then
3. Introduce your own ideas

Use the Four S's

Even a good book can be better when the reader uses the Four S's—Say Less, Stress, Go Slow, Show. Think of your reading as a performance in which you can draw your child in with your voice, actions and facial expressions. If you can, use different voices for each of the characters.

Say less by substituting words and phrases your child understands. Books with appealing stories will sometimes be too long or complicated for your child. So don't just read the story as it's written. Break down complex sentences into smaller parts.

Stress important words—especially tuning-in words—the way an actor would, to make them more interesting and meaningful. (To review tuning-in words, see Chapter 5.) Make an unfamiliar word stand out by saying it with emphasis, explaining its meaning and then using it again in a different sentence. For instance, if the word "stubborn" comes up, as in the sentence "He was a stubborn boy," you could say something like, "He never changed his mind" (explanation), immediately followed by, "What a stubborn boy!" (using the word again in a different sentence).

Go **S**low enough for your child to follow the story. Make sure you pause every now and then, waiting silently to give him time to think about what he's heard, look at the pictures and add his own ideas. Remember too that slowing down can create suspense at just the right spot.

Show your child what the words mean. Point to the pictures as you talk about them or run your finger under the text as you read. Make sure your child knows who all the pronouns ("he," "she," "him," "her," "they," "their" and so on) refer to. Show him who you're talking about by adding the person's name or pointing to the picture. Add some specific information to remind him what's already been said about the "he" or "she" in the story.

Look how Ali's father reminds him who's doing the talking in the story:

Dad checks to see whether Ali knows that "he" refers to Matthew, the little boy in the book.

Once in a while, ask your child a question about a picture but don't show it to him. When he can't answer, say something like, "Oh, I'm sorry. I forgot that you need to see the picture to know what it is." Then turn the book toward him so he can see that seeing leads to knowing.

Don't worry if your child wants to read the same book over and over. But make sure you read it in different ways so he won't get stuck on just one way. If the book has introduced him to a new word, try to use it in other conversations, too, so he'll have many opportunities to learn it.

Read to Help Your Child Tune in

The ideas in the stories you read together offer natural starting points for conversations with your child. To teach him more about tuning in, take him into the minds of the characters in the book.

Use your I's (Include, Introduce, Insist)

Many children's books are about people wanting or liking things. For example, *Red Is Best*, by Cathy Stinson and Robin Baird Lewis, is a simple tale about a little girl whose favourite colour is red. *Bread and Jam for Frances* (mentioned in the book list above) tells the story of a girl who only likes to eat bread and jam, until she sees her friend eating a more interesting lunch. Think of the classic fairy tales. In *The Three Little Pigs* each pig prefers to build his house out of a different material: sticks, straw or bricks. Goldilocks has to taste every bowl of porridge until she finds the one she wants to eat. All of these situations offer opportunities for you and your child to talk and think about how everyone looks at the world differently.

Photograph albums help your child remember the past. You can both talk about how people in the photos felt, what they wanted and what they were thinking when each picture was taken.

Look. Your sister's crying in that one. Do you remember why she's crying?

She wanted my ice cream.

Talk about what the characters think and feel

Books often feature characters whose feelings are open to interpretation. Point to the pictures that illustrate emotions and ask your child questions like, "How do you think she's feeling?" or "Why do you think she's angry?" Give your own opinion, and don't always agree with your child.

In some books the characters themselves have different ideas from one another. For example, in the fable *Seven Blind Mice* (as retold by Ed Young), a gigantic, unknown object turns up at the pond one day. Each of the mice tries to figure out what the strange thing is. (It's an elephant.) Find opportunities like this one to use "think that" in your sentences ("He thinks that it's a snake"), and encourage your child to talk about the book in the same way ("What does the green mouse think that the trunk is?").

Find a character whose reaction is unexpected. For example, a story might show a father offering to take his daughter to the zoo, but the girl is sad because she really wants to stay home and play with her new friend. Challenge your child to think about why the girl is unhappy.

Encourage your child to think along with the characters in the book by pausing before turning a page and saying, "I wonder what he's going to do next." Try some storybooks without words. They naturally encourage conversation about different ways of interpreting what's going on in the story. Books with hidden pictures, such as the *Where's Waldo?* series, let you both *wonder* and *think* about where Waldo is and *remember* where you saw him last time.

Dad lets Jack tell him what he thinks the snowman's eyes are made from. Then he gives his own opinion.

Talk about different points of view

There are so many different ways to look at a book, and they're all opportunities to have a conversation with your child. For instance, when the pictures don't match what the characters say, point it out to him. When the book presents a problem, talk about various possible solutions. ("I think we should turn the page, even though Grover says not to. What do you think we should do?") Usually you and your child will be able to think of more than just the one solution offered in the book. Your child might also have had an experience like the one the character is having but handled it differently.

Talk about how things aren't always as they appear

Point out the parts of a story where a character says he's doing one thing while he's really doing something else. For example, in the fairy tale *Little Red Riding Hood*, the Wolf tells Grandmother that he's her granddaughter come to visit. Later, he tells Red Riding Hood that he's her grandmother. Help your child understand that the Wolf is telling lies. Other great liars of the fairy-tale world include Pinocchio, the Boy Who Cried Wolf and just about all the characters in *The Emperor's New Clothes*, who tell the Emperor they like his clothes while he walks around naked.

Talk about characters' false beliefs

Just about any book gives you an opportunity to compare what the characters believe with what's really going on and how these beliefs shape the characters' actions. Books that are built around a false belief make it even easier to have this kind of conversation. For instance, while reading the fairy tale *The Emperor's New Clothes*, you could say something like, "The Emperor thinks he's really wearing clothes." For *Good Night, Gorilla*, you can show your child that people sometimes hold false beliefs with comments such as, "The zookeeper doesn't know that the gorilla let all the animals out" or "The gorilla's really *tricking* the zookeeper."

Talk about solving problems

So many books show how characters use various strategies to solve problems. For example, in *King Bidgood's in the Bathtub*, the king's servants and friends try various strategies to coax him out of the tub. Use your list of contrast words to highlight how each character tries something different. Say something like, "Everyone has a *different* idea of how to get the king out of the bath." (To refresh your memory of contrast words, see page 75.)

Link the book to your child's life

Help your child see how the book connects to his life. Compare and contrast the events, actions and feelings in the book to those your child has experienced. For example, if you talk about how the green mouse is afraid of the "snake" in *Seven Blind Mice*, you might say something like, "Remember how you felt when you saw a snake on our camping trip?"

Keep Adding New Ideas

Talking about what the characters are thinking and feeling is just one way to stretch your child's thinking with books. A few other ideas follow.

Talk about the past and future

Using the book as a starting point, you can talk about the past ("Look at how the children dressed a long time ago") and the future ("I wonder where she's going to look for her baby now"). When you stop and ask your child "What happens next" (for books he's familiar with) or "What do you think will happen next" (for books he's unfamiliar with), he can make predictions and think along with the character. If your child is ready for more challenging questions, ask him to help find solutions for the character's problems.

Mom asks Luke to help solve the monster's problem. To do this, he has to think about what the monster might do next.

Give background and details

Remember to give your child the background knowledge he needs to appreciate the story. Start by showing your child the book's cover and talk about what the story will be about. Right from the beginning, your child can think about what the book means to him. For example, if you're about to read *Franklin in the Dark*, you might say, "This is a book about Franklin being afraid of the dark. Are you afraid of the dark?"

Explain words that are unfamiliar, add some details or explanations to make the story easier to understand and always try to relate what's happening to your child's life.

She's his mother, but she's very old now. And her little boy is all grown up. Now it's the boy's turn to look after his mother.

Mom gives James an explanation not written in the book, so he understands the meaning of the story.

If you use story-telling words to set the scene (such as "once upon a time") or to emphasize the progress of the plot ("the next thing that happened" or "the end"), your child might eventually use them in his own stories. Hearing these words repeated often in a variety of books is the key to his learning their special function in stories.

Add imagining and pretending

Have some puppets or props handy as you read, so you and your child can easily take on the roles of characters in the book. At first your child might want to stick to the story as it's written. Try to encourage him to add something new. Use the last two I's from your I-Cues: Introduce a new idea and then playfully Insist on follow-through.

Hey brothers. Let's have lunch. That wolf is never coming back.

No, Mommy. That's not in the book!

At first Jack resists when his mother changes the story to introduce something new.

Little pigs, let me in. No eating lunch now!

Then he decides it's fun to come up with a new idea of his own.

Let Your Child Do the Reading

There are two skills your child needs to read aloud: he has to know what sounds the letters make, so he can decode the words, and he has to understand what he reads. Some children with social communication problems find recognizing words and sounding them out easy. There is even a small group (about five to ten percent of these children) who read at the age of three or four years, which is much earlier than most other children. For this last group, understanding what they read is the challenge. Others find decoding more difficult and need to work on both reading and comprehension.

Children who learn to read will quickly discover a whole new way to find out about the world and the people in it. If you think your child may be ready to learn this skill, these kinds of books may make the learning easier:

> Books that make some words stand out in talk bubbles or in signs
> Books featuring often-repeated words or phrases, so your child can memorize them—For instance, in *Brown Bear, Brown Bear, What Do You See?* by Bill Martin Jr., the sentence "What do you see?" is repeated over and over so that your child can eventually recognize the line as soon as he sees it.
> Rhyming books

Make print "talk" at home

One of the best ways to encourage your child to become a reader, besides reading books together, is to make print a part of his everyday life.
Here are a few tips:

> Point out simple messages on signs and billboards, such as "STOP" and "McDonald's." (Your child will probably point out that one to you!)
> Look at the TV guide with your child. Point out the titles of his favourite shows before selecting them. Let him guess what you're going to watch by reading the words.
> Look at the credits after a TV show or video ends and encourage him to read some of the names. This will be easier if he's familiar with the characters.
> Watch TV shows that encourage reading. *Sesame Street* and *Wheel of Fortune* are favourites with children who love the alphabet.
> Make cards for special occasions and let your child do the printing. Don't be concerned with his spelling. Let "pza" work for "pizza" for now.
> Put a calendar of events on the refrigerator and refer to it each day.
> Write notes to your child and help him read them aloud.
> Ask for children's menus with pictures and help your child choose what he wants.
> Read the instructions to games and the covers on videos, and follow diagrams together to assemble new toys.

Notes on the refrigerator show your child the importance of print.

As you read books to your child, run your finger under the words. Show him how changing one letter can change a whole word. (For example, "funny" becomes "sunny" when you change the F to an S.) When your child can recognize some easy letters (such as D, F, P and M), ask him to guess what one or two words are that begin with those sounds. Rhyming books are helpful at this stage.

Remember that sounding the words out is just the first step. He needs to understand what he's reading. So when your child reads for himself, ask him the same kinds of questions that you did when you were the reader ("What do you think will happen next?").

Another option is computer reading programs. Many of your child's favourites (such as Arthur and Little Critter) are available in the Living Book series, found on-line. Look for programs that go beyond just having your child match a word to a picture. Find the ones that show how the word works in sentences.

And remember: if your child is very good at sounding out words, he might start reading books that he doesn't understand. As a rule, the books your child should read by himself are the ones in which his reading-aloud ability is at about the same level as his understanding.

• •

The best way to help your child tune in to what's on the minds of other people is to give him a lot of opportunities to hear and talk about their thoughts and feelings. Reading books with your child gives him plenty of opportunities to project himself into someone else's mind and learn about the world.

In most of this chapter, you took on the role of the main story-teller. But the more you read to your child and tell him other people's stories, the more he'll be motivated to tell stories himself. In the next chapter, you'll learn other ways to help your child take that leap.

Help Your Child Become a Story-Teller

Together, James and his mom tell the story about the last time they took a walk on the bridge. By asking the right question and adding a bit of the information, Mom helps James tell part of the story, too.

Stories like this one have a special place in conversations. When someone tells a story, there is a meeting of minds between speaker and listener. A well-told story makes it possible to see events through someone else's eyes.

No one is born a story-teller. It takes a long time to become one, and your child will need your ongoing help to get there. If you and he have been reading books together (Chapter 7) and talking about the past (Chapter 6), then he's already off to a good start.

What Successful Story-Tellers Do

Daniel's story is hard for his mother to follow.

I C E   Michael and Daniel are trying to tell the same story about what happened at school, but only Michael is successful. That's because his story has a clear beginning, middle and ending, and he explains who said and did what. Michael knows how to **"ICE"**: **Initiate** the story, **Continue** it with details and and then **End** the story.

Let's take a closer look at how Michael's story works. First, he sets the stage by announcing his intention to tell a story ("I want to tell you what happened today..."). He gives some specific details so that his mother will know exactly where the story happened ("at school") and who it's about ("us kids" and "Mr. Berg").

Michael's story is easy to follow because it has a clear beginning which leads smoothly to a middle section, which in turn leads to a clear ending ("So we went out"). Along the way, he gives explanations for why things happened ("because it was raining") and how people reacted ("no one wanted to go out").

Daniel, on the other hand, doesn't introduce his story. He launches into it without giving his mother any background information (for example, he never says who the "he" is). He also includes a detail that has nothing to do with the story ("I saw a pothole with water in it").

It's hard to follow Daniel's story because he lists the events without explaining what they have to do with one another. He also seems to lack some of the vocabulary of basic story-telling. For example, he wants to quote his teacher, but instead of saying, "Mr. Berg said that there was no more bingo," Daniel calls his teacher "he" and then just repeats what Mr. Berg has said, word for word ("No more bingo").

To be a successful story-teller, Daniel needs to learn how to make it easy for the listener to follow his story. That means he has to know how to introduce his story and how to use the right words to keep the story going all the way to the end. In Chapter 3 you learned that the ability to ICE (initiate, continue and end) is an important skill in conversation. Good story-telling also depends on knowing how to ICE. You'll learn more about ICE and its relationship to story-telling as you read on.

What Types of Stories Do We Tell in Conversations?

There are two types of stories that come up in conversations: formal stories and casual stories.

Formal stories

The formal story is structured and follows a set of rules. For example, one rule is to present the events in the order they happened in. Another rule is to describe how a problem that arises in the story gets solved. (You'll find all of these rules explained below.) Michael's story about what happened at school on a rainy day is a formal story because it follows these rules.

It will take a long time for your child to learn to tell a formal story from beginning to end all by himself. To guide him in the right direction, you'll need a good understanding of the rules a formal story follows.

Rules for Formal Stories

To tell a formal story, the story-teller must:

1. **Initiate** the story by giving important background information

2. **Continue** the story by:
   - Describing the events in a logical order
   - Giving explanations for emotions, thoughts and actions
   - Using specific vocabulary
   - Making the story interesting by acting like a character, adding details or emphasizing words
   - Explaining why the story is important to him/her

3. **End** the story by bringing it to a conclusion

1. **Initiate the story by giving important background information**—This means that the story-teller sets the stage for the story right at the beginning by explaining who it's about and where and when the story happened.

2. **Continue the story by...**

   ... describing the events in a logical order—A good story-teller usually describes a story's events in the same order they happened in. That way, the story has a clear beginning, middle and ending. The "high point" of the story (the most important part) doesn't have to come at the end. It can even come near the beginning ("I was riding and I fell off my bike, and then...").

   ... giving explanations for emotions, thoughts and actions—Explaining why things happen makes a story easier to follow. For example, "We stayed inside because it rained" tells us more than just, "We stayed inside." As we saw in Chapters 5 and 6, understanding why people feel or do something gives the listener a window into their minds.

   ... using specific vocabulary—"Linking" words (for example, "because," "if/then," "when," "before/after" and "so"), "contrast" words (such as "before/now," "now/later" and "but") and "communication" words (such as "say" or "tell") all help glue the story together. There are also some tried-and-true phrases for opening a story. Early story-tellers might say, "Know what?" "Remember when...?" or "I want to tell you about...." Experienced story-tellers might begin with "Listen what happened..." or relate their story to the ongoing conversation by saying something like "That reminds me of...," "Speaking of..." or "By the way...."

   ... making the story interesting: acting like a character, adding details or emphasizing words—Even the best story will be boring if the story-teller doesn't tell it well. It's up to the story-teller to change his or her voice, add sound effects and keep the listener entertained (a good story-teller uses the Four S's).

   ... explaining why the story is important to him/her—There are a few ways to make certain parts of the story stand out as the most important. The story-teller can:
   - Talk about feelings ("I was sad," "Was I ever mad!")
   - Stress specific words by exaggerating or repeating them ("It was a *bad* movie," "It *really* hurt," "I was crying and crying")
   - Give more details for emphasis ("My knee was bleeding. It was bleeding on my pants")

3. **End the story by bringing it to a conclusion**—In general, a story ends with a description of the event that happened last. This event might be the high point of the story, but often it isn't. When a story describes attempts to solve a problem, the ending should state how the problem was or was not solved. A story can also end with an opinion about the story ("That was the most fun I ever had").

Look at how Jack in the pictures tells his story about falling off his bike. Notice how he uses the rules for telling a formal story. He gives background information telling the listener who the story is about and when and where it happened. He describes the events in the order in which they happened, building his description to a high point (falling down). As he tells the story, he lets us know how he feels about what happened.

What happened to your leg?

He gives background information.

I was riding my bike. And I didn't see the rock. And I just bumped into it and falled down.

He describes the events in order and builds the story toward a high point: falling off his bike.

You fell down. And then what happened?

What?

I was crying and crying. And Brad's mommy came running. And you know what?

He lets us know his feelings.

All the parents came. And someone put a Band-Aid on my leg.

He gives his story an ending.

Casual stories

Most of the stories that children tell as part of a conversation are not formal stories but casual ones, with fewer details. A casual story follows some of the rules of a formal story, but not all of them.

Often there's no formal beginning to casual story-telling because all the necessary background information is already familiar to everyone. For example, as you and your child talk about other things, one of you might be reminded of something interesting that happened in the past. Or perhaps an event in a book or a TV show makes one of you think about something similar that happened in real life.

Often these casually shared stories move quickly from the past to the future. This is likely to happen as one or both of you make a plan for the next time something like that happens.

Adam and his mother tell a casual story about his soccer game. Their story started out being about the past and ended up being about the future.

What Are Children's Stories About?

All of the children's stories described in this chapter so far come from the children's own experiences. These personal stories are different from fictional stories, which are usually based on a movie, a TV show, a book or an idea that comes from the story-teller's imagination.

It's good for your child to practise telling both kinds of stories. Remember, however, that relationships between people depend on their sharing their own personal stories with each other.

Personal stories

In personal stories, you talk about yourself—about things that happened to you in the past or that might happen to you in the future. Parents tell these kinds of stories to their children at all stages of their childhood. And children, even those who are obsessed with videos or computer games, try to tell personal stories often.

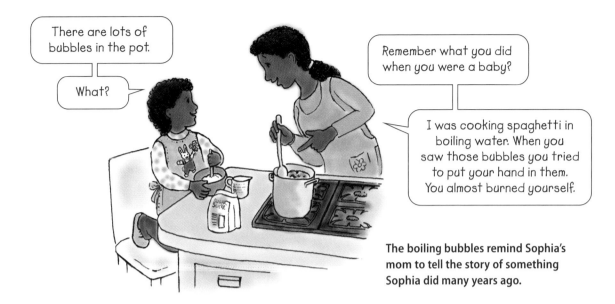

The boiling bubbles remind Sophia's mom to tell the story of something Sophia did many years ago.

Fictional stories

Fictional stories often retell all or part of the story of a movie, a book, a TV show, a computer game or even a joke. It's probably easier for your child to tell these kinds of stories than to make up his own. Books and movies are prepackaged with all the necessary ingredients; someone else has already made up the beginning, middle and ending of the story. Because movies and books can be replayed or reread, your child has visual images to remind him how to tell the stories. If your child loves a character from a TV show, he's probably eager to tell you everything that character has done or said.

Some children repeat fictional stories from memory, word for word. While rote story-telling is fine in the beginning—a good start, even—keep in mind that eventually your child should learn to tell all stories in his own words. And with a little encouragement from you, your child might eventually make up his own fictional stories and put some characters from books or TV into them.

Early Story-Tellers

Not many young children tell stories that follow all the rules, as Michael and Jack have done earlier in this chapter (though Jack had some help from his mother). Early story-tellers make different kinds of attempts to tell stories before they are completely successful. While far from perfect, these first tries let you know that your child wants to share his experiences with you.

Keep reading to find out what kind of story-teller your child is now. With a clearer understanding of what he can already do, you'll also have a better idea of what the next steps for him might be.

The list story-teller

Early story-tellers often just list the events that happened, not always in the order in which they occurred.

There was cake and there was presents and there was ice cream and there was a clown and there was cake.

Emily tells her story by naming all the things she saw at the birthday party.

The short story-teller

Children's early stories can be short and lacking in detail, especially background information that the listener needs to understand what's happening. Sometimes the short story-teller repeats the same thing over and over.

Here's an early story from Ben about his fishing trip with his father. In it, Ben only tells two things about the experience (the fish was big and he put it in the boat).

Mother: Did you and Daddy catch a fish?
Ben: Yes.
Mother: You caught one?
Ben: It was a great big one, and I lifted it up. I lifted it up in the boat.
Mother: Really? Right up in the boat?
Ben: Yes.
Mother: Wow.
Ben: I lifted it in the boat.

The hopping story-teller

This story-teller hops around from event to event in a way that's confusing to the listener. Listen to Dylan go from one thought to another as he tries to tell his father what happened when he fell off his bike. (Compare his story to the one Jack tells on page 123 about a similar accident.)

My leg bleeded. My bike smashed. There was a rock.

Dylan hops from one thought to another as he tries to tell his mother what happened when he fell off his bike.

The monologue story-teller

While some children don't give enough information, others might give too much. For example, your child's idea of a story might be to tell you everything he knows about his favourite topic without stopping for air. Or he might provide way too much detail about something that bothers him (for example, how his card collection isn't in the usual order).

Be a Story-Telling Model

Before your child can tell any stories, he needs to hear you tell your own stories. If you make a habit of sharing the interesting things that have happened to you, your child will start to pick up some of your story-telling skills. In other words, you'll be a good model to your child.

So, as often as you can, talk to your child about the past—both the distant past and the recent past. As you do so, emphasize all the story-telling elements that he needs to learn. For example, if he rarely talks about his feelings in his stories, make sure you do in yours.

And remember that it's not always what you say, but how you say it. Keep the Four S's in mind—Say Less 😊 (use straightforward simple language), Stress 🖤 (emphasize key words, change your voice to reflect how people feel), Go Slow 🐢 (give your child time to process) and Show 👆 (show emotions on your face and with your body actions).

Look how Christopher's father talks to him about his feelings so that Christopher will do the same when he tells his own stories.

Grandpa gave me this hammer a long time ago. We made a birdhouse with this same hammer. I really love this hammer because Grandpa gave it to me.

Help Your Child Tell the Story with You

There are two basic ways for your child to tell a story: he can tell the whole story by himself or he can tell it with you. Sometimes he might want to do all the telling himself, especially if his story is about one of his special interests or if it's from a video he's seen. But keep in mind that, during conversations, children don't usually tell complete stories on their own. That's because it's more fun and much easier for them to tell their stories with the help of a supportive parent.

When you help your child tell a story, you add the missing parts. You can also ask him just the right questions, to encourage him to hold up his part of the story. Eventually, you'll want him to be able to tell stories on his own, but this isn't the goal you should have in mind right now.

For the time being, concentrate on co-telling—telling stories with your child. That means the two of you will share the story-telling, taking turns to tell little bits of the story.

Co-telling works best if the two of you have shared the experience that you're talking about. The possibilities for stories are endless: a family vacation, a funny thing that happened at dinnertime, an incident at a birthday party, a family outing to the zoo, a meal at a restaurant or your child's first ride on a train, a plane or a bus. Young children especially love to remember about things that went wrong, so consider experiences such as a bee sting, a fall from a bike, the time the dog ran away or the day you locked yourself out of the house.

Use a responsive style

Having a responsive conversation partner can make or break a child's ability to tell a story. Look at how differently these two mothers talk to their children and how their children's stories are affected.

Deb gave me pushes on the swing.

Pushes on the swing. Wow!

First she pushed Jade, and Jade went high. I didn't go high.

Maybe Deb got tired, so she couldn't push you hard.

I think she got tired. But it was fun.

When Jack's mom follows his lead, he tells a pretty good story about his day at the park.

Did you go on the swings?

Did you play with Caitlin?

Did you have lunch?

Yeah.

Yeah.

Yeah.

Mark's story never gets told because his mother just asks him question after question.

Jack's mother follows his lead and includes his words when responding to him ("pushes on the swing"). Her first comment is just "Wow!" It shows her interest and is meant to encourage Jack to continue the story without giving him too much help. It works: Jack takes another turn ("First she pushed Jade..."). Then Jack's mother adds an idea of her own to the story with a comment about why Jade's swing might have gone higher ("Maybe Deb got tired, so she couldn't push you hard").

In contrast, Mark's mother doesn't ask any open-ended questions or add interesting details to the story. Notice how quickly she changes the subject from talking about the swing to asking about lunch. As a result, Mark takes the same number of conversational turns (three) as Jack but says only "Yeah" each time. He never tells his story.

Use your I-Cues

Being responsive means using your I-Cues to help your early story-teller (for an I-Cue review, see Chapter 4). Read on to find out how the I-Cues can guide you in making story-telling a back-and-forth experience for you and your child.

Include your child's words and interpret

Use the first "I"—Include your child's interests, ideas and words— to let your child know you're listening to him and agree (or disagree) with what he has said.

Use the second "I"—Interpret— when your child can't come up with something to say or when what he says is unclear (for example, when he leaves out important information or tells the story's events out of order).

You can help your child fill in missing details by repeating back what he has just said (including his words) and then saying it the way he would if he could (interpreting). That way he gets a model of how to tell his story. Remember to stress 🖤 the parts that he's left out by changing your voice and saying the new part slowly 🐢.

Mom uses some of Dylan's own words and then adds the parts of the story that Dylan has left out.

Insist on having your turn

There are some children (monologue story-tellers) who want to take all the turns and never give you a chance to talk. That's okay once they're able to tell an interesting story from beginning to end. But if your child gives too many details or goes on too long with his story-telling, try to get your two cents in by taking a turn that will make the story more interesting. If that doesn't work, help him move on by insisting on having a turn. You can use some of the same ideas you tried when conversations and book discussions became one-sided:

Use a gesture, action, facial expression or words to hint that it's time to change directions—For example, look away from your child or look at your watch. If those actions alone aren't enough, explain to your child that looking away means you're not interested any more and that he should wrap up his story soon. Perhaps you can work out a secret signal with your child, such as holding your hand up to indicate when his turn is over or putting your index finger to your mouth in the "be quiet" sign.

Use a visual cue—Sometimes, holding up a cue card that says something like "Wait" or "My turn" lets your child know that he should give you a turn to talk.

Be direct—Warn your child that after he says one or two more things about his topic, you expect him to talk about something else.

Focus on the positive—Every so often comment on how you like your child's waiting and listening.

Cue your child to take a turn

More often, though, early story-tellers need encouragement to take their turns in the story-telling. Your Cues will let your child know when and what he's expected to add to the story.

Take your child's ability to tell stories into consideration when you cue him to take his turn:

If your child needs a lot of help...
You might end up telling most of the story for your child if he can't. That's okay because he'll learn a lot from your model. But he won't get any practice telling stories if you're the only one talking. To help a child who needs a lot of help:

> Use visual cues—It might be easier for your child to tell a story if he can see some photographs of what happened.
> Include his words to let him know you're listening
> Interpret (say it as he would if he could)
> Add comments that develop the story
> Ask easy-to-answer closed questions ("Who," "What" or "Where" questions) or ask a tag-on yes/no question
> Hint at what he could say ("I wonder what Daddy did with the camera")
> Make a suggestion ("You could tell me where you went after the party")

Daniel needs a lot of help to tell his story. Look how his mom uses Cues to make it easier.

If your child needs less help…

Once your child can hold his own in telling the story, you can do and say less.
To support a child who needs less help:

> Include his words
> Comment and wait
> Ask open questions—For example, "What happened next?" or "Why?"
> Hint to remind him of something else he can say

For all children…

You should be prepared to use several kinds of Cues to help your child
continue the story.

Did you and Daddy catch a fish?

You caught one?

Really? Right up in the boat. Wow!

Yes

I lifted it in up the boat.

It was a great big one, and I lifted it up.

Mom's easy-to-answer questions keep Ben in the conversation, but he doesn't add many ideas to his story.

Asks open question

What happened next?

Daddy took the hook out of the fish.

Mom's open question helps Ben continue the story

Comments and makes a suggestion

There's no fish in the bag. Tell Mommy why.

We threw it back in the water.

Dad's Cues help Ben remember the rest of the story.

Keep on Telling Stories Together

You might think that you should stop helping your child tell stories once he gets the hang of it. But it's best to keep telling stories together even after he starts telling them on his own. If you continue to share the story-telling, you can help him tell even better stories, with more details and new ideas.

Let's return to Jack's story about falling off his bicycle but, this time, take it a step farther:

Mother: What happened to your leg? (She asks an open-ended question.)
Jack: I was riding my bike. And I didn't see the rock. And I just bumped into it and falled down.
Mother: You fell down. And then what happened? (She asks another open-ended question.)
Jack: I was crying and crying. And Brad's mommy came running. And you know what?
Mother: What?
Jack: All the parents came. And someone put a Band-Aid on my leg.
Mother: I'm glad someone had a Band-Aid, aren't you? (She talks about her feelings and then asks an easy-to-answer question.)
Jack: Yeah. I'm glad someone had a Band-Aid, so I didn't get blood all over my pants. (Jack uses his mother's model to talk about his own feelings and then adds a new idea.)

Jack's mother helps him tell the story about falling off his bicycle by asking him a couple of open-ended questions. Knowing that Jack rarely mentions how anyone feels in his stories, his mother emphasizes the importance of talking this way. Her comment with a tag-on question, "I'm glad someone had a Band-Aid, aren't you?" gives Jack a model and lets him sort out his emotional reaction to his cut ("Yeah. I'm glad someone had a Band-Aid"). This detail encourages Jack to add more information to his story ("...so I didn't get blood all over my pants").

. . . .

Learning to tell a story within an ongoing conversation takes a long time and a lot of practice. Don't expect your child to tell stories by himself right away. He'll need you to guide him and to add interesting details for a long time. Remember to:

> **Talk frequently about the past with your child**
> **Keep the story on topic**
> **Encourage your child to say more about the topic**
> **Let your child know when he's said too much**
> **Let your child know what you need to know**
> **Use your I-Cues**
> **Balance your questions and comments**
> **Give the right amount of help to encourage him to take his turn**

You probably won't see results immediately, so be patient and guide your child toward better story-telling one step at a time.

9

Make the Most of Make-Believe

Walk into any preschool classroom and you'll see children playing "doctor," "house" or "school," or pretending to be their favourite action heroes. When children play with their peers in these imaginary situations, they form friendships and practise their social and language skills.

In this chapter, you'll learn how to stretch your child's imagination and help him discover the joy and very real benefits of make-believe.

The Power of Pretending

Make-believe—or "pretend play"—is first of all about having fun. Just by using his imagination, your child can change the real world into anything he wants it to be. He can really go to the zoo or he can just pretend to go. He can eat the banana he's holding or pretend it's a telephone.

But pretending is also about learning, and there are many important lessons that can be learned from this kind of play. For example, because the real world and the world of make-believe exist side by side, pretend play helps children get used to the idea that things aren't always as they appear to be— a banana can become a telephone and you can go to the zoo without ever leaving home.

Pretend play is also a wonderful way for children to tune in to the feelings and thoughts of others. When your child pretends to be someone else, such as Mommy, Daddy or a firefighter, he has a chance to "stand in the shoes" of another person and see the world from that person's point of view.

When your child starts to enjoy playing make-believe with you or with another child, he'll soon find out that people don't always imagine the world in the same way. He'll have a first-hand opportunity not only to use his own mind to pretend, but also to watch a more experienced pretender (you) think out scenarios. Some of your responses might surprise him and make him think about the make-believe situation in a different way. For instance, maybe your little pig wants to build his house out of ice cream or your Goldilocks decides to bypass the Three Bears' house and visit the mall instead.

Creating an imaginary world often requires teamwork. That means that while children play, they have to take the ideas and feelings of their play partners into consideration. They need to decide who's going to do and say what. Not everyone can be the director or the hero of the story. As children develop their make-believe, they learn to express their desires, co-operate and work out problems.

Find out what kind of pretender your child is

Pretend play develops over time. Sometimes a child might seem very advanced in one area (maybe he reads or can name all of the planets in the solar system) but isn't pretending the way you'd expect him to. He may have some pretend skills but not others.

When you find out what your child can and can't do, you'll be ready to help him get lots of practice pretending to be other people—complete with their own thoughts and feelings. Let's look at the stages of pretending to see which one your child might be at now.

Not a pretend player

Some children don't pretend at all. They might only like to play with toys that don't lend themselves easily to pretending, such as puzzles and computer games. Or they might play with toys that other children use for pretend play (for instance, stuffed animals and action figures), but they don't use these toys in an imaginative way. They never make their animals talk or pretend to be someone else.

Early pretend player—Pretends with real or realistic objects

The first way your child might pretend is by copying something he has seen you do in everyday life. In this early stage of pretending, he'll probably use real objects or realistic-looking toys. For example, he might hold the telephone to his ear and say, "Hi! How are you?" or borrow your camera and put it up to his eyes as if to take your picture. He may even move his toy car along the floor while making some motor sounds.

The same skills that are important in helping your child tune in to the thoughts and feelings of others are also important in early pretend play. At this stage of play, your child has to do two things:

> Pay attention (tune in) to you so he can copy what you do
> Understand when you're pretending—For example, he interprets your smile, special look and actions to mean that you're not really going to eat his hand; you're just pretending.

Early dramatic player—Acts out familiar scenes

Perhaps your child acts out scenes from real life. When children do that, they usually start with scenes they're very familiar with. For instance, a child at this stage of pretending might put his stuffed animal to bed, kiss it and then turn out the lights, just as his mommy and daddy have done for him all his life.

For many children, fiction is another rich source of make-believe. Children with ASD or AS often have excellent memories and can remember whole chunks from television shows or books. If your child has that kind of mind, he might act out a story from a book or a movie exactly as he's seen it. He may even be quite unhappy if you try to change it. While this kind of pretending might not seem very imaginative, it can be a starting point for more creative play.

You'll know that your child's play is becoming more imaginative when he stops reproducing scenes exactly as he's seen them. He might also begin to act out less familiar scenes, such as a visit to the doctor or the hairdresser. At this stage, his play will be quite simple, without a real story line. His doctor may examine a sick stuffed animal with a toy stethoscope, take its temperature and then give it a pill.

It's a big step forward when he wants you to play a part in his make-believe. He'll take on the role of doctor or hairdresser and make you be the patient or customer. By this time, your child shouldn't need to use objects that look exactly like the real thing. If he's pretending to be a doctor, he might give you a flu shot with a pencil or cut your hair using his two fingers as scissors.

Emily can imagine that the blanket is a hairdresser's cape and that she's holding a blow-dryer in her empty hand.

Around the same time that your child begins playing with these imaginary toys, he'll probably start using some simple language to develop the play. For example, he might say what he's going to do before he does it ("I'm going to put Bear to sleep") or speak for his toys ("Wah-wah-wah! I'm a hungry baby!"). He may also talk about where the toys should go ("Let's put the barn here").

As your child acts out familiar scenes with you, he needs to pay attention and tune in to you to copy what you say and do. When acting out familiar scenes with you, your child must also learn to do these things:

> Understand that you can play with something that you create with your mind
> Understand that he can play with something that he creates with his mind
> Understand your ideas about the play (for example, he knows when you're pretending to be someone else)
> Accept or not accept your ideas about the play (for example, he feeds the bear after you suggest it or tells you the bear isn't hungry)
> Share his ideas about the play with you (for example, he tells you what he's planning)

Social-dramatic player

This kind of play always involves playing with others. In its most highly developed form, it looks like a real dramatic performance because there is a plot with a beginning, a middle and an end to it.

In early social-dramatic play, your child might act out simple stories like shopping at a grocery store or playing house. As he becomes more imaginative, he might look beyond his everyday experiences for ideas and pretend to be a monster hunter or a superhero battling his evil enemy. To play at this level, your child will need to be able to communicate with others. To do that, he'll need the right words (see chart below).

With the right words your child can...

...plan and create the make-believe:

> He can act and talk like the person he's pretending to be or what he wants his toy to be ("Help! Help! My house is on fire!").

> He can direct the play by describing who should do what ("I'll be the fireman, and you be the mommy" or "Let's pretend you're only a baby").

> He can develop the plot of the story ("I'm Billy Blazer and you're a baby, and I'm going to rescue you").

> He can tell his play partner what he wants the objects to be ("This string is a dog leash").

> He can describe actions that won't be acted out ("There was a fire, so you called the fire trucks").

...tune in to his play partner:

> He can problem-solve and negotiate with his play partner ("We can't both be firemen. I'll be the fireman first and you be the fireman after").

> He can agree or disagree with his play partner's suggestions ("Yeah, let's pretend the string is a leash" or "Good idea!").

> He can build on the ideas of his play partner. (If his play partner says, "Here's a cow," your child can do or say something to follow this lead, such as bringing another cow into the play and saying, "Here's another cow.")

> He can ask his play partner his opinion ("What's this thing for?" or "It's the leash, okay?").

Let's say the skipping rope is the fire hose.

Oliver can use language to create a fire hose from a skipping rope.

The Pretend Play Checklist

On page 152 you'll find a checklist to help you learn what kind of pretend play your child can do right now. Recognizing your child's stage of pretending will give you an idea of what skills he has and which ones he needs to work on.

Expand Your Child's Pretend Play

There's more to getting your child to pretend than just putting out some interesting toys. How much your child learns about pretending depends a lot on you. So get ready to be a real playmate by keeping one thing in mind: play is supposed to be fun!

Read on to find out how you can set the stage to make your child's pretend play more successful.

Give your child real-life experiences

One way to help your child learn to pretend is to make sure he has many experiences to draw from. It's easier to play at being a zookeeper or a hot dog vendor after a visit to the zoo or lunch at a hot dog stand.

How long can we keep this book?

Bring it back in two weeks.

First, Luc and his mother go to the library...

How long can I keep this book?

Bring it back in two weeks.

...and now that Luc knows something about what librarians do, he can pretend to be one with his mom at home.

Provide the right toys

The play materials your child has will influence his pretend play. So try to have some toys and objects at home that are similar to the things he sees in real-life situations. For example, after a visit to a restaurant, bring home a menu or make one with your child, and take out the toy dishes and pretend play food. Now you're both ready to play restaurant.

Gracie's father makes his restaurant look like the real thing with toy dishes, an apron and an order pad.

Besides having toys and props that match his real-life experiences, your child should have toys and objects that match his stage of play.

Toys for early pretend play

The best toys for a child who isn't yet pretending or is just starting to pretend are either the real objects or toys that look a lot like the real thing—for example, toy telephones. Other good ideas: a toy shopping cart, realistic-looking food and real grocery store bags; dishes, pots, pans and a child-size toy stove, sink and refrigerator; a baby doll, doll clothes and a bottle; or some of Mommy and Daddy's clothes (such as a hat, a tie, shoes or a purse). Puppets seem to appeal to children at all stages of play.

Toys for early dramatic play

If your child is new at this kind of play, stick with realistic toys. Toy cars, trucks, trains and a floor mat with city streets on it are always a hit. Think about themes when getting your toys and props together. For example, children can play zoo with plastic or stuffed animals; pet store with a cash register and a few of your cat's or dog's toys; doctor with a toy stethoscope and thermometer; or school with paper and pencils.

You can also find things in your cupboards to stretch your child's imagination. For example, he can build a pretend bus from large boxes; turn pillows into a fort; fill a car with gas from a skipping-rope hose; go fishing with a long string; or pretend a large pot is a drum. Puppets, props and costumes—such as an apron, a restaurant menu, a chef's hat, a fire hat or your old clothes—can all inspire him to create the make-believe.

As your child's play becomes more imaginative, try some miniature versions of things; objects that don't look exactly like the real things; or imaginary toys that you create with your actions (such as bringing your empty hand to your mouth as if you were holding a cup). If your child has trouble using less realistic objects to stand for something else, you'll find some ideas on the following pages for what to do.

Does this bus go to Finch Avenue?

Yes it does, lady. But no babies on the bus today!

Boxes are perfect for making forts and buses.

Props or toys that go with a favourite video or book can also trigger your child's pretend play. Remember, though, that if your child gets stuck acting out the same story over and over, his imagination isn't getting a workout. When that happens, try introducing new toys to expand the story. If that doesn't work, you might have to put the props that go with the video or book away and then introduce a new theme with different toys.

Toys for social-dramatic play

If your child is able to engage in more advanced make-believe play, you can use all the toys already mentioned as well as toys that he might not have as much experience with: action figures, dinosaurs, spaceships, a superhero's cape, masks or a toy sword. Keep in mind that his play with new toys might not be as advanced as his play with more familiar ones.

In social-dramatic play, however, toys and props aren't really necessary. Your actions and words can create them ("Let's pretend you're holding a shield and it has magical powers").

At times, your child might be more interested in the way a toy looks, feels or sounds than in using it for pretending. For example, while playing grocery store, he might get stuck pushing the buttons on the toy cash register over and over. If something like that happens, put the distracting toy away for a while.

How many toys?

Too many toy choices can be overwhelming for some children. If your child flits from one activity to another, put all other toys away when you want him to focus on pretending. If the toy food, the play money and the cash register are the only things he sees, he's more likely to play pretend store.

The TV and the computer might be big distractions for your child. If that's the case, keep the pretend toys in a different room when you can.

Have duplicates of some toys so there will be one for your child and one for you. This is a good strategy for a child who is just starting to pretend. He'll find it easier to copy what you do with your toy if he has the same one himself.

You'll be glad to have duplicate toys when other children come over to play. Having two of your child's most prized possessions is one way to avoid arguments with his friends.

Join in with your child and add something new

No matter how your child plays, you can help him develop more advanced pretend play and language by joining in with what he's doing and then adding something new. Joining in is different with children at different pretend stages. Basically, though, it means following your child's lead by getting involved in what he's interested in at the moment.

For example, if he's moving a toy train along a train track, get down on the floor with your own train and move it near his. Once you're part of the play, model something new that your child can respond to. For instance, stop your train and say, "All aboard!" or "End of the line. Everybody out!"

If your child is new to pretending, he might simply copy you. If he's a more experienced pretender, he might decide to add something new to the play, too.

Dad's pretending gives Caleb an idea of something else to add to the play.

All aboard!

All aboard. Hurry up! We have to get to Grenadier Station.

Play like a child

You'll be more interesting to your child, especially during social pretend play, if you play the way children play. That means acting and sounding, not like Mom or Dad, but like the character you're pretending to be.

If your child resists your joining in, keep "the Two P's" in mind: be playful and persistent.

Read on to find out how joining in works with children at different stages of pretending.

Join in when your child isn't pretending yet—to develop his early pretending skills

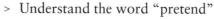

When your child isn't pretending at all, getting him to the next stage depends entirely on his copying of what he sees people do in real life. That includes copying you as you pretend.

Here are some goals for you to keep in mind for your child as he becomes familiar with pretend play. You want your child to:

> Understand the word "pretend"
> Understand when you're pretending and when you're not
> Use realistic toys or real objects to pretend
> Pretend to do some things that happen in his everyday life

To begin, play beside your child. Get your own toy and imitate what he is doing. So if he's pushing his toy car along the floor, get your own car and do the same thing.

Beep-beep! You're driving too slow.

For a child who isn't pretending yet, watching you model this new kind of play is the best way for him to learn. So find opportunities throughout the day to demonstrate make-believe. For example, when your child is having a snack, ask for a bite of his cookie and then pretend to take one. Have a puppet or a stuffed animal do the same thing. Puppets can drink from your child's cup, take pretend bites from toy food and give thank-you kisses.

Highlight your make-believe by describing what you're doing. For example, if you pretend to have a conversation on a toy telephone, say something like, "I'm not *really* talking to Grandma. I'm *pretending*." Or when you bite into an imaginary apple, try a comment like, "This isn't a *real* apple. It's a *pretend* apple." Stress ♥ the words "real" and "pretend" and show 🖐 your child with a smile that there's not going to be any actual eating.

Join in when your child has started pretending—to help him act out familiar scenes

If your child can pretend but is stuck on performing one or two repetitive actions with a toy, join in and model some new skills.

Here are some goals to keep in mind for a child who's doing some pretending with real objects or realistic toys. You want your child to:

> Act out some familiar scenes
> Use objects that don't look exactly like the real things
> Act and talk like the person he's pretending to be
> Talk about his pretending
> Accept or reject your ideas about the play
> Share his ideas about the play with you

The possibilities for you to add new ideas to the pretend play are endless. If, for example, your child just drives his train to the pretend station, stops quickly to pick up a new passenger and then repeats the same scene again and again, you'll know it's time to join in and add something new. You could grab a toy figure and become the passenger who wants to buy a ticket. Or you might place a toy animal on the track, forcing the "conductor" to blow the train's whistle.

Remember that by being playful and persistent, you can help your child stretch his imagination a little further. For example, in the picture shown on the next page, James doesn't understand when his mother pushes him around in his chair, pretending it's a car. But she refuses to give up. She keeps on pushing the chair and talking to James as if he's behind the wheel of a speeding vehicle.

Honk the horn, James. We don't want to run Stitch over.

Beep-beep! Move over, Stitch!

Mom keeps the "car" speeding around the room until James finally understands the make-believe.

Remember to make yourself sound like the character you're pretending to be—take on the squeaky voice of a baby or bark if you're pretending to be the dog.

Join in when your child acts out familiar scenes—to develop his social-dramatic play

If your child is pretending to be his father or mother, his teacher or a store-keeper by copying some actions or repeating a few things these people might say, he's ready for social-dramatic play. At this point, he can start developing the skills introduced in the social-dramatic play section.

Plan and create the make-believe by...
> acting and talking like the person he's pretending to be
> directing the play by describing who should do what
> developing the plot of the story
> telling his play partner what he wants the objects to be
> describing actions that won't be acted out

Tune in to his play partner by...
> problem-solving and negotiating with his play partner
> agreeing or disagreeing with his play partner's suggestions
> building on the ideas of his play partner
> asking his play partner his opinion

Use this list as a guideline for helping your child move into social-dramatic play. (To review examples of the items on the list, see page 139.)

Social-dramatic play develops gradually. Again, it's up to you to move the play forward by joining in and adding something new.

If this kind of play is still new to your child, concentrate on helping him to act and sound like the character he's pretending to be and to develop the plot. When your child is beginning to get comfortable with this kind of play, focus on just one or two goals at a time during your pretending (see the list of "plan and create" skills and "tune in" skills on the previous page). Here are a few more points to keep in mind.

Rehearse before playing

At the beginning, your child might find it hard to develop a plot and think of things to say right on the spot. By reading a book or watching a movie first, he'll have some ready-made ideas for pretending afterwards.

If he wants to stick to the story just as he's heard it, introduce something new as soon as possible. For example, in the picture below, see how James's mom persuades him to play along with her story change.

Mom makes a suggestion that isn't in the story. At first, James doesn't like her idea, but she persists so playfully that James can't resist joining in.

Stay in the role

Your child is more likely to stay in his role if you stay in yours. For example, instead of saying, "T-Rex is hungry," take the dinosaur and use your scary dinosaur voice to say, "Arrgh! I'm very hungry! And I like the taste of little bears."

Remind your child to stay in his role by speaking to him as if he were a monster, a train conductor or a bear, but not your little child ("You can't get away from me, little bear. I'm the mighty T-Rex").

Both Emily and her mother have the most fun when they talk and act like the characters they are pretending to be.

Step outside the play

Sometimes your child needs more help than you can give him while you're in your pretend role. If your child doesn't respond to you while you're in character, you might have to be Mom or Dad for a moment, offering a suggestion for what he could do next.

When you have to step outside the play, change your voice back to your natural one to ask a question, give a hint or make a suggestion that will get the play back on track. Then quickly return to the make-believe.

Mom's question reminds Sarah that she's supposed to sound like a monster, not like Sarah.

Now Sarah uses her monster voice to tell her mother what to expect next.

Join in when your child is a more experienced social-dramatic player— to develop creativity, flexibility and tuning-in skills

Even when your child is able to act out stories, he needs to practise stretching his imagination and opening his mind up to new ideas, especially those that aren't his own. Helping your child become flexible in his play is one of the best ways to prepare him for making friends.

Let's look at how one mother helps her child develop his creativity. Eric, shown in the page of pictures on the right, likes to play pretend grocery store. His mom's goals are for Eric to come up with some new things his grocer can say and to be able to take turns when he plays.

Whenever Eric and his mother play grocery store, they play the same way over and over: Mom asks how much the food costs and Eric tells her. It's time to make the pretending more imaginative.

Mom hints that she needs help. When Eric doesn't respond, she asks more directly. Then Eric comes up with a new idea: charging her more. Next time they play this game, he might decide to carry her bags.

Eric's mother wants him to learn that he can't always be the grocery man. She negotiates with him.

Then, for the next five minutes she stays put behind the cash register and treats Eric like he's the customer, not the grocer.

Working out problems during play

Problems can come up during pretend play that have nothing to do with pretending. For example, we've seen that Eric has trouble giving up the cash register to his mother. He insists on being the grocer even though his mother wants to exchange roles with him. In this case, giving a warning and then being playful and persistent work.

Here are some problems that might occur when you play with your child (and at other times too!):

> He wants to take all the turns.
> He doesn't want to share a toy.
> He wants to play longer than you do.
> He insists on playing his way.
> He gets distracted.

You can use these difficult situations as opportunities for your child to practise problem-solving. If by some miracle you don't encounter problems when you play with your child, then create some. Working out problems with you will prepare him for working out problems with other children. (There will be more about playing with other children in the remaining chapters.)

Solutions to problems aren't always easy to find. Here are a few tips to help you, some of them based on ideas you've already read about in this book.

Tips for Problem-Solving

> **Plan ahead to avoid problems later.** This might mean talking with your child first about what's going to happen in the play, so he won't be unpleasantly surprised by any part of the make-believe. Also, try to minimize the things that you know upset or distract him. For example, if he often turns on the television when he's trying to avoid doing something new, don't play near the television.

> **Use problem-solving words,** such as **now/later** (as in "You can be the fireman now, and I'll be the fireman later"); **is/isn't** a good idea (as in "It isn't a good idea to put all the cars on the ramp"); **some/all** (as in "You can be the fireman some of the time, not all of the time"); **same/different** (as in "Let's play a different way"); **or** (as in "You could give me a turn now or take one more first"); and **share** (as in "Let's share money. You can have all the dollars and I'll have the coins"). It's a good idea to use these words in other situations first (for example, "You and I like different kinds of fruit"), so your child can practise using them when he's calm and relaxed.

> **Focus on the positive.** You'll have better results if you let your child know when he's doing something right rather than just correcting him when he's doing something wrong. For example, think about Eric, the boy who wants to be the grocer all the time. His mom should resist saying to him, "I don't like it when you don't take turns" and instead compliment him when he does co-operate: "I like it when you take turns with me." The positive approach boosts his self-esteem and encourages him to take turns again.

> **Talk about how people are feeling.** Encourage your child to identify his and your reactions and emotions both when all is going smoothly ("You're fun to play with," "I like it when you listen to me") and when you run into trouble ("I feel sad when you shout").

> **Talk about consequences.** Help your child think about the probable results of what he's doing, so he can adjust his behaviour ("If I try Dad's idea, he'll want to play again").

> **Teach your child something different to do or say to replace socially unacceptable behaviour.** If, for example, your child throws toys or shouts when he gets angry, you could teach him one of the following stress relievers (or a combination of them): take a deep breath, count to 10; walk away; say "I'm angry" or "Darn it!" in a calm voice or ask to play something else. When you sense an outburst coming on, remind your child about the more appropriate reaction ("Count to 10" or "Walk away") before he has a chance to do what he's used to doing.

> **Help your child figure out what else he can do.** There's always a choice in every problem situation ("Is there another way you can tell me that you want to stop playing?"). Try to give your child some control in finding a solution ("Do you want to take a break now and play some more later?").

> **Use a visual helper to work out the problem.** Using a hand signal (such as holding your index finger in the air to tell your child to wait or making the okay sign when he does something you like) can help you keep your child on track while focusing on the positive. Also try writing down some key reminders on cue cards (such as "There's more than one way to play"). (We'll discuss other kinds of visual helpers in Chapter 13.)

> **Choose your battles.** Sometimes, it's better to ignore mildly annoying things that your child does (such as insisting he always use a certain colour toy) and concentrate on having fun. You can always work on those issues at another time.

Let's look at how Eric's mother could have used these tips to help Eric if he had continued to insist on being the grocer.

Pretend Play Checklist

Put a check mark in the box that describes how your child pretends and write an example in the space provided below.

○ No pretend play

Some early pretend play

○ Copies someone else who is pretending
Example:

_____

○ Pretends with real or realistic toys and objects
Example:

_____

○ Understands when someone is pretending
Example:

_____

Early Dramatic Play—Acts out familiar scenes

○ Acts out scenes from videos or books
Example:

_____

○ Acts out scenes from everyday life
Example:

_____

○ Pretends with objects that don't look exactly like the real thing
Example:

_____

○ Pretends with imaginary objects
Example:

_____

○ Includes a play partner in the pretending
Example:

_____

○ Talks like the character he's pretending to be
Example:

_____

○ Describes what he's doing
Example:

_____

Pretend Play Checklist continued

Social-Dramatic Play

Planning and creating the make-believe:

○ Acts and talks like the character he's pretending to be
Example:

_____

○ Directs the play by describing who should do what
Example:

_____

○ Develops the plot of the story
Example:

_____

○ Tells you what he wants the objects to be
Example:

_____

○ Describes actions that won't be acted out
Example:

_____

Tuning in to his play partner:

○ Works out problems
Example:

_____

○ Agrees or disagrees with his play partner's suggestions
Example:

_____

○ Builds on the ideas of his play partner
Example:

_____

○ Asks his play partner for opinions
Example:

_____

When you and your child create imaginary worlds together, such as make-believe restaurants, hospitals or grocery stores, he has a chance to try on different roles: to be the waiter, the doctor or the grocer. Besides giving your child a chance to think and talk like those people, this kind of play is preparing him to play the same pretend games with other children. In the next chapter, we'll turn our attention to your child and his relationships with playmates of his own age.

10

Know Your Child's Friendship Skills

Most children make their first friends when they are preschoolers. They discover that it's fun to have a pal to run after or to splash in puddles with. They also learn that they have to share and compromise, or else their new friends might not want to play with them any more. In other words, if your child wants to keep his playmate, he'll have to tune in to his playmate's feelings.

Luckily, in these early years you'll be more involved in your child's social life than at any other time. That means you'll have many opportunities to help him learn how to play with other children and make friends.

This chapter will help you identify what friendship skills your child already has and which ones he still needs help in developing.

What Are Your Child's Social Play Skills?

Sometimes you just "click" with another person. That person usually shares some of your interests and, more importantly, likes you as much as you like him or her. It's the same with children. But liking someone isn't enough to get a friendship going.

To make friends, your child needs some special skills. He needs to know how to initiate play with another child. He has to be able to continue playing by taking turns, sharing his toys and talking with the other child. And he needs the ability to consider the other child's opinions and feelings. We call these skills "social play skills" because they are ordinarily learned through play with others.

Of course, children develop these skills gradually as they grow. Your child may be behind other children in learning these skills, but with your help he can probably get better at them, learn to enjoy playing with other children and even make new friends.

You might think that your child prefers to play alone, when in fact he simply hasn't discovered how to join in and play with other children. Even children who are verbal and sociable can find the world of their peers overwhelming. But all children benefit from social play, and most will enjoy it thoroughly when they know what to do.

The first step in helping your child is to find out how he's playing with other children now, so you'll know what he can and can't do. Start by taking the following quiz to get a better picture of your child's social play skills.

Social Play Skills Quiz

In this quiz, "other children" can mean just one other child or any number of children.

	NEVER	SOMETIMES	OFTEN
1. My child plays alone.	○	○	○

	NEVER		SOMETIMES		OFTEN	
	With one other child	With a group of children	With one other child	With a group of children	With one other child	With a group of children
2. My child plays near other children. He watches them but "does his own thing" with his own toys.	○	○	○	○	○	○
3. My child plays beside other children, using the same toys as them. He might smile at another child, copy something that child does or borrow a toy.	○	○	○	○	○	○

		NEVER		SOMETIMES		OFTEN	
	Social Play Skills Quiz continued	With one other child	With a group of children	With one other child	With a group of children	With one other child	With a group of children
4.	My child joins in physical play with other children (such as running, chasing or going down the slide).	○	○	○	○	○	○
5.	My child plays turn-taking games with other children (such as board games or hide-and-seek).	○	○	○	○	○	○
6.	My child teams up with other children to make things (for example, a fort out of pillows, a tower out of blocks).	○	○	○	○	○	○
7.	My child pretend plays with other children (such as playing grocery store or restaurant).	○	○	○	○	○	○
8.	My child initiates play with other children in an unusual way. (For example, he might take a toy away from another child, walk up and hug a child without warning or ask an unusual question like, "What kind of vacuum do you use?")	○	○	○	○	○	○
9.	My child initiates play with other children by joining in with their activities (for example, he approaches another child and starts playing with the same kind of toys).	○	○	○	○	○	○
10.	My child initiates play with other children by commenting on the play (for instance, saying something nice to them such as, "I like your fort").	○	○	○	○	○	○
11.	My child builds on the ideas of his playmate(s). (For example, when another child builds a tower out of blocks, your child might add a block to it. Or when his friend suggests playing school, your child might say he wants to be the teacher.)	○	○	○	○	○	○
12.	My child talks with his playmate(s) (probably only a few times during one activity) as they play together.	○	○	○	○	○	○
13.	My child works out problems with his playmate(s) as they play together.	○	○	○	○	○	○
14.	My child tunes in to the feelings of his playmate(s).	○	○	○	○	○	○
15.	My child tells his playmate(s) when he's had enough of the game they're playing.	○	○	○	○	○	○

Most children start down the path to friendship by identifying one special person whom they want to be with. All a child really needs in the beginning is one best friend with whom he can "hang out" and practise his social skills.

If you noted in the quiz that your child has some social play skills but only when he plays with one other child, he should continue to play one-on-one. Even a child who shows many social play skills will benefit from continuing this kind of play. But a child with many skills is also ready to start playing in groups of three or more.

Three Levels of Social Play Skills

The remaining chapters in this book will discuss strategies to improve your child's social play skills. For now, though, what's important is understanding how these skills develop naturally through play. As you read the rest of this chapter, use your quiz answers to identify your child's current level of social play. Then keep reading to learn which skills he still needs to develop.

No social play skills

If you wrote in the Social Play Skills Quiz that your child **often**...

> Plays alone (#1) or
> Plays near another child or a group of children (#2)

... then your child probably doesn't know what to do or say to join in with other children.

Sometimes, children play alone because they want to play their own way. They may find it hard to do what someone else wants. An "often" or "sometimes" answer to question #2 lets you know that even though your child plays alone, he's interested in other children; he just needs some help in getting in on the action and staying there.

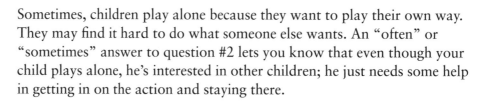

Sam is interested in other children but doesn't yet know how to play with them.

Goals for a child with no social play skills

If your child doesn't seem to be interested in playing with other children, he may need to spend more time with them simply by being in the same room. After observing another child play for a while, he's likely to become more comfortable with the idea of joining in.

If your child already shows an interest in what other children are doing, then he's probably ready to start moving toward the next stage. That means, first, playing beside other children and sharing toys. They're not really playing together just yet, but it's a good start. (For example, they each build their own tower using blocks from the same box or move their own trains back and forth on the same set of tracks.)

Then your child will be ready to join in some play with one or two other children. Activities that the children can do in unison, like singing songs or moving to music with one another, help build friendships at this stage. When you notice the children exchanging glances and smiles, you'll know they're starting to connect. Other activities your child may start to enjoy at this stage include sharing physical activities (such as chase or running after a soccer ball).

These kinds of play will help lead your child to the next stage. In the beginning, though, the goals for a child with no social play skills are to **stay and play beside another child** (or other children). Playing briefly beside another child— or even just being in the same room—is the first step. To summarize . . .

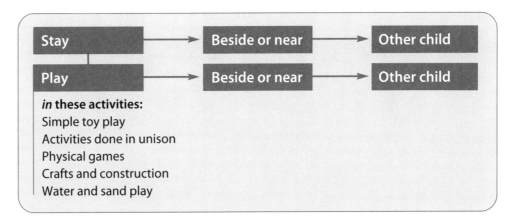

Don't expect your child to stay with another child throughout the entire play date. In the beginning, he might join his friend for one or two activities out of five. Consider it a bonus if the children talk to one another.

Some social play skills

If you wrote in the Social Play Skills Quiz that your child **often** . . .

> Plays beside another child or a group of children, using the same toys as them (#3) or
> Joins in physical play with another child or a group (#4)

or **sometimes** . . .

> Initiates play with another child or a group by joining in with their activities (#9)

. . . then your child is already starting to make friends. Playing alongside another child is a good stepping stone to playing together. Your child is learning what to do by watching others play.

A child with some social play skills often enjoys physical play with other children, such as running beside a friend, jumping into pillows together, kicking a ball around with each other or jumping on a trampoline together (or the bed, if it's allowed). He also joins in with other children in activities that they can do at the same time. For example, if he knows the words to the song, he'll sing along with other children or move his body to music when they do.

At this stage, if your child is next to his friend enjoying an activity like drawing with crayons or building something with blocks, he might share his crayons or blocks with his friend. Or he might ask his friend for something he needs for his own creation. But don't expect a lot of conversation between your child and his playmate. View the odd request for a toy or a comment from your child about the play as a real plus.

Sam has taken a big step forward by playing beside another child.

Goals for a child with some social play skills

Your social play goals for your child will depend on how long he already stays and plays with another child. If his time spent in social play is short, your goal should be extending it. One way is to increase the number of social play activities in his playtime—turn-taking games and teamwork activities, for example (more on these in Chapter 11).

Once your child is enjoying playing with another child, conversation should take off naturally. For starters, he's going to have to respond to his friend's comments and questions. He'll probably want to talk about the play, too, by adding his own comments about what's happening. Next, he'll need to learn to say things like, "It's your turn now" and "The big block goes here." Keep in mind, though, that children don't usually talk to each other the whole time they play together. Expect them to say something to each other about five times during each play activity.

A child with some social play skills is ready to start acting out make-believe stories with his friend. In this kind of pretend play, your child must share his ideas with his friend to make the pretending work. After all, you can't run a pretend restaurant if no one can agree on who should be the customer and who should be the waiter.

When children with some social play skills want to initiate play with another child, they often just join in the play. If you answered "sometimes" or "often" to question #9, you'll know that joining in with another child's activity is how your child shows he's interested in playing with another child. If you answered "sometimes" or "often" to question #8 ("My child initiates play with other children in an unusual way"), then your child probably wants to make friends but doesn't know how. He might position himself near another child and hope this child will include him. Or he might grab or throw a toy to get the other child's attention or say something silly. None of these approaches will be welcomed by the other child.

Your child needs to replace those kinds of behaviour with some more socially acceptable conversation openers. Saying "Can I play with you?" is better than grabbing the other child's toy. But research shows that the best icebreakers are either giving a compliment or making a positive comment on what's happening.

Saying something nice to someone is the best way for your child to initiate play.

Hey, Daniel. That's a cool tower!

To summarize, the goals for a child with some social play skills are to **initiate play by saying something positive**, and then to **stay and play, talking every now and then with the other child**.

Initiate play		
Stay and play	**+**	**Talk *with* the other child**
in these activities:		*for* these reasons:
Physical games		To respond to his friend's questions/comments
Turn-taking games		To ask his friend a question
Teamwork activities		To comment on the play
Activities done in unison		

Many social play skills

If you wrote in the Social Play Skills Quiz that your child **often**...

> Plays turn-taking games with another child or a group of children (#5)
> Teams up with another child or a group to make things (#6) or
> Pretend-plays with another child or a group (#7)

...then your child is already well on his way to building friendships. He understands turn-taking in games (but might not always like it). He can be part of a team that is organized around a goal. He is comfortable with social-dramatic play, taking on a role and telling his friend what each of them should do.

Now that he can take turns, plan and talk with another child, Sam is definitely on his way to making friends.

If you said in the quiz that your child **often**...

> Initiates play with another child or a group of children by joining in with their activities (#9)
> Initiates play with another child or a group by commenting on the play (#10)
> Builds on the ideas of his playmate(s) (#11)
> Talks with his playmate(s) as they play together (#12)
> Works out problems with his playmate(s) as they play together (#13)
> Tunes in to the feelings of his playmate(s) (#14) and
> Tells his playmate(s) when he's had enough of the game they're playing (#15)

...then you can stop reading—your child has superior social skills. However, most likely you answered "never" or "sometimes" to more than one of the above questions (or you wouldn't be reading this book). Even the most verbal and sociable children often get stuck in their play when they have to work out problems and take their friends' feelings into consideration.

Goals for a child with many social play skills

At this stage, you'll be helping your child learn any skills that he's missing and increasing how often and how well he uses the skills he already has. For instance, he can learn more complex pretend play, in which he uses language for all of the purposes discussed in Chapter 9 (see page 139 for a reminder). And this is the time for him to become a better playmate by doing more talking and more tuning in to his friend's feelings.

Now that your child is used to playing with another child, the focus will be on the way the two children talk to one another. That means that your child will have to remember to consider his friend's feelings by asking him what he wants to do or how he wants to play. He needs to understand that if he wants to keep his friend, he's going to have to accept some of his friend's ideas, even when he likes his own better. And he needs to learn that you don't just walk away when you don't want to play any more. You need to tell your friend what you're doing.

Maybe your child is fine playing with another child as long as things are going his way. When problems come up, however, he might not know how to talk them through. Instead he may choose a physical solution (such as pushing) that may anger his playmate. So even a child with a lot of social play skills needs to work on his negotiating ability.

In summary, the goals for a child with many social play skills start with **tuning in to his playmate**. Then he'll be able to **build on the playmate's ideas** (for example, he'll see his friend making a tower out of blocks and add one of his own blocks, or when his friend suggests that they pretend a cardboard box is a boat, he might give his friend a towel to use as the boat's flag). He'll also be able to **agree or disagree with his playmate** and to **work out problems** (such as who goes first in a game). And he should also be able to **end the play** by telling his friend he's had enough or wants to play something else.

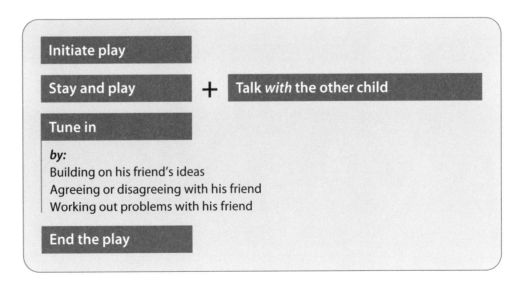

Initiate play

Stay and play   **+**   Talk *with* the other child

Tune in

by:
Building on his friend's ideas
Agreeing or disagreeing with his friend
Working out problems with his friend

End the play

. . . .

This chapter should have given you a good idea of the kind of playmate your child can be right now. Keeping his strengths in mind, you're ready to invite another child over for a play date. So read on to learn how to prepare yourself and your child for this next step.

Be Your Child's Play Coach

11

The more opportunities your child has to get together with other children, the more comfortable he'll be with them. But just inviting another child over for a play date won't be enough. You must take an active role in guiding your child's play with other children. The next three chapters of this book will tell you how.

In this chapter you'll read about all the things you can do to make your child's play dates more successful even before his friend knocks on your door.

The Three Parts of Coaching

Before you invite another child over to play, help your child feel comfortable around other children by taking him to places where you're bound to run into them. Visit playgrounds, parks, petting zoos and even toy stores or family restaurants. When you meet other children in places like these, give your child a model of how to be friendly by smiling and greeting some children every now and then.

Once you decide to have more formal play dates, you'll need to take a more active role. Think of yourself as a coach, helping when the "players" need you to keep the play going and standing on the sidelines when all is going well between the children. There are three parts to being your child's play coach:

> Set up the play
> Step out and stand by (while the children play together)
> Step in (when the children need your help)

The second and third parts will be covered in Chapter 12. For now, let's concentrate on the first.

Set Up the Play

Planning is everything. When arranging a play date, there are several things you can do ahead of time to help the play date be more successful.

Find a friend for your child

In looking for the right friend, ask yourself these questions:

> Do the children like one another?
> Do the children have similar interests?
> Will the other child ask your child to join him in play?

Your child's first friend should be friendly. That means finding a playmate who will respond to him, share some of his interests and hold up his end in the play. After all, your goal is for your child to experience social success. By playing with a sociable child, your child will have a good role model to learn from.

If you need help finding a play partner, ask other people who are involved in your child's life (such as his teacher or babysitter) to suggest a child who could be a friend for yours.

On the following pages, we'll discuss a few more points to consider when choosing a friend for your child.

How many friends?

It's easier for your child to play with one friend at a time. When he can form strong relationships with one or two children individually, he'll be more ready to join in with groups of children.

What about siblings?

A sibling can be an excellent first friend for your child. By developing the relationship between your child and his brother or sister, you will help build a lifelong friendship. Just by being in the same family and sharing much of the same history, your child already has a lot in common with his sibling.

Don't be put off by arguments between siblings. All friends have disagreements. An angry brother or sister can teach your child a lot about respecting another person's point of view. If your child learns how to work out problems with his family first, he'll be better prepared to make and keep other friends.

Christopher knows he's going to have to find another way to get a turn playing with his sister's toy.

What age should friends be?

For different reasons, your child may benefit from playing with children who are younger or older. If your child is very reluctant to socialize with other children, you might try finding a friend for him who is a year or two younger. A younger child will probably look up to your child, making him feel more like a leader than a follower. As your child becomes more sociable, you can find playmates closer to his age.

On the other hand, an older child can model play skills that are new to your child, such as how to talk problems through or how to use language to plan the play. In the end, what probably matters most is the attitude the two children have toward each other and whether they share the same interests.

Does it matter if it's a boy or a girl?

Research shows that little girls and little boys often play and talk in different ways. Because he can learn different things from each group, your child should have practice playing with children of both sexes.

 Knowing how boys and girls play and talk, however, might guide you in choosing a playmate, especially in the beginning when your child is just starting to make friends.

Boys as friends

Boys generally don't focus much on tuning in to the feelings of others when they play together. Instead, they spend a lot of time in physical play, and a lot of boy talk is about planning activities. For example, they might talk about how they will build a fort or play a game or do something they're not supposed to do.

Boys take turns being the leader, but there is also a lot of one-upmanship going on when boys play together. Challenges such as "I can run faster than you" are common. In a boy's world, it's natural for friends to boss each other around and not give explanations. They don't feel a need to explain why they think they're the strongest, the fastest or the smartest. They just are.

To win approval from his friends, a boy may say a rude word or do something naughty. Good manners aren't that important to most preschool boys. When they want something, they often push or shove to get it. When boys play with girls, however, they tend to be more willing to "play nice."

When boys play together, be prepared for some bragging and some rude words.

Girls as friends

Girls, on the other hand, tend to be more interested in sharing their thoughts and feelings. They spend a lot of time talking about who they like and who likes them. Often, a favourite conversation topic is the things they've done together, such as sleepovers and birthday parties.

Little girls like to talk about things they've done together in the past.

> **When choosing a first friend for your child, remember:**
>
> > A boy's feelings might not get hurt as easily as a girl's
> > if your child "tells it like it is."
>
>
>
> We're going to play house. You be the daddy.
>
> That's stupid.
>
> > A girl can be a good friend for a boy who needs direction.

Pick a place and a time

To make sure that your child is relaxed, invite another child to your home. If the first play dates are at your house, you can control the environment. That means you can put away a lot of toys so there aren't too many distractions. You can also limit most of the play to one room, making it easier for the children to be close together. Once the children are comfortable playing with one another, move the play date to the other child's home. Your child needs to get used to playing at his friend's house too.

Try to have some idea ahead of time how long the children should play together. Keep in mind that longer playtime isn't necessarily better playtime. It's best to end the play date when your child and his friend are still having fun. That way, both children will have good memories of their time together and look forward to seeing each other again. While you can't know exactly how long the fun will last, early play dates should usually be between one and two hours long. So discuss the drop-off and pick-up times with the parents of your child's friend before they arrive at your house.

Include unstructured and structured playtime

Sometimes the best play isn't planned. *Unstructured* playtime is "hanging out together time." The beauty of it is its spontaneity. Children who don't have rules forced upon them often invent their own to get along with each other.

So make sure your child and his playmate get some unstructured playtime. This kind of play is especially important when children are just getting to know one another or are only starting to develop an interest in other children. The first thing each child needs to learn is that his new friend is fun to be around.

One way to set up unstructured playtime is to put toys out at the start of a play date and just let the children do their own thing, without any pressure to play together. Another way is to let them chase each other in the backyard and then have lunch or a snack together. Having them sit side by side to watch a video also counts as unstructured play—even if they don't talk to one another.

Watching a movie together is a good way to start a friendship.

Structured playtime—time set aside for play that you plan and supervise—is less open-ended. During structured play, you should expect your child to stay and play with his friend and possibly talk to him, too. As you'll see later in this chapter, some toys lend themselves more naturally to a "my turn–your turn" kind of relationship. But you can turn any activity into an interactive one with some planning.

Create teamwork

The best activities for getting children to play and talk together are ones that require teamwork, where each child has something specific to do in order to reach an end goal. Here are a few ideas:

Some Ideas for Teamwork Activities

> **Making a snack** such as a sandwich, pudding, cupcakes, juice or chocolate milk—Each child has his own job to do. For example, one child can pour the milk and the other one can then put the chocolate into the cup.
> **Baking** cookies or a cake
> **Building** a fort or tower with blocks or pillows—After the children build the pillow tower, they can jump into it.
> **Acting out a situation** with pretend-play toys

Even putting a puzzle together or using a shape sorter can become a teamwork activity if you set it up that way. For example, have one child be the "keeper" of the puzzle pieces or shapes. The keeper is in charge of holding and handing the pieces to the other child, who completes the job.

How you present a teamwork activity to your child and his playmate will affect how much they'll play with and talk to one another. When you put out the toys (or whatever they're playing with), you basically have three approaches to choose from: give no information about what to do with them, give some information or give detailed instructions. Your choice will depend on the level of social play skills your child has. To understand this choice better, read on.

No social play skills

| If your child has no social play skills and your goal is to have your child STAY and PLAY with similar toys *beside* his friend ... | → | Put out the toys but *give no information.* |

Setting up an activity this way gets children who play alone used to playing beside other children and using the same toys. So put out the toys, such as blocks or puzzle pieces, and let the children do whatever they want with them. (For more information on toy selection, see "Choose the right toys and activities" on page 172.)

This approach can benefit even more sociable children. There's no pressure to play a specific way, and therefore each child can use his own imagination. Without any structure, however, children might end up working alone on their own creations with very little interaction. If your goal is for the children to talk to each other, try one of the other suggestions described below.

Just putting out toys with no instructions gives children a chance to get comfortable with one another.

Some social play skills

| If your child has some social play skills and your goal is to have your child STAY and PLAY *longer*... | → | Put out the toys and *give lots of information.* |

When children are told exactly what to do, they will often stay until they get the job done, so this approach is a good one if your child needs to work on playing longer with another child. Ask the children to make something, such as a tower or a puzzle, and show them what it should look like. Then tell or show them exactly how to make it. (You could give them a step-by-step guide with pictures.) Keep in mind that while the children concentrate on completing an activity, there won't be much talking between them. That can come later.

Many social play skills

If your child has a lot of social play skills, and your goal is to have your child STAY, PLAY *and* TALK to his friend...

→

Put out the toys and *give a little bit of information.*

Knowing what to do but not how to do it gets children talking to one another. So ask the children to make something and show them what it should look like, but don't tell them how to do it. When you present toys in this way, your child and his friend will probably team up to figure out how to make something together. Without specific information from you, they might figure out who should do what and work out a plan together (such as, "You put all the blue ones on and I'll do all the red").

When it comes to pretend play, your child and his friend might do better if they already have an idea of what they can say and do to make the play more interesting. So discuss or rehearse it with them first. (You'll read more about this on page 174.)

Choose the right toys and activities

Large toys and play equipment, such as swings, slides, trampolines, ride-on toys for two and wagons, are ideal for unstructured play. So are balls, bowling games, basketball and hoop, blocks, jumbo puzzles and drawing supplies.

Make sure you know ahead of time what kinds of toys the other child likes. Sometimes it's easier to get play going between the two children if your child greets his friend with a toy that is one of the other child's favourites.

Children who are just getting used to being with other children can play beside one another. More experienced players can take turns or work out their own games.

It's your turn, Sam.

Look for toys that are more fun for two children to play with than one.

Think about your child's sensory preferences, too. If your child needs to move to feel calm and focused, make sure there's some time for active games.

The kind of pretend-play toys your child will enjoy the most depends partly on his stage of pretend play. A child in the early stages of pretending needs realistic-looking toys, like life-size baby dolls, ride-in cars, child-sized gas pumps, stoves, sinks and toy telephones. If your child is more experienced at make-believe, he'll like both realistic and miniature toys. Many children, especially boys, enjoy playing superheroes. So have some capes, shields and swords on hand, too. If you provide toys that your child is familiar with, he'll already know some things to say and do with them. (See Chapter 9 for more discussion of pretend-play toys.)

If your child's goal is to stay and play without a focus on talking to his playmate, plan an activity in which he and his friend can do something in unison, such as singing a song, painting a mural, looking at photographs, playing musical instruments or moving to music.

Singing songs is a good way to keep children together.

If you're happy and you know it, clap your hands...

Games with rules, such as bingo, checkers or Snakes and Ladders, have turns built right into them and often have a colourful game board that makes playing easy to understand. Good interactive games don't have to cost a lot—or anything at all. A game of catch features turn-taking and a specific way to play. So do hide-and-seek and "What Time Is It, Mr. Wolf?"

What time is it, Mr. Wolf?

Two o'clock.

This game is a good one because the players know exactly what to say when it's their turn to sneak up on the wolf.

When you shop for board games or computer games, look for ones that have simple rules and opportunities for turn-taking. Games in which there are no winners or losers are available in stores. While most children like computer games, conversation can be limited during this activity. So think of being on the computer as unstructured playtime when your child and his friend can relax and enjoy each other's company.

Here are some tips to keep in mind when putting toys out:

> **Don't put out too many toys at one time.** Think about putting away the ones that your child might find hardest to share.
> **Put out toys that your child already knows how to use.**
> **Have duplicates of your child's favourites.** Having two of the same toys will help avoid arguments and make it easier for your child to copy his friend.
> **Think of things that your child can share with his friend,** such as drawing on an oversized piece of paper, using one box of crayons, placing wooden beads on a single strand of string or eating a snack from the same large bowl.
> **Think of ways the children can use the toys to play together** (such as taking turns or making one person the keeper who gives his friend what he needs—such as blocks or glue—when he asks for it).

Too many toys can spoil the fun.

Sometimes having one toy or one piece of paper results in teamwork.

Discuss or rehearse the play before it starts

When arranging a play date, set the stage for success by making sure your child and his friend know what to expect. You can do this by going over what's going to happen in the play date. As you'll see below, there are certain things that you can rehearse with just your child and others that you can talk about with both children present. If possible, let the other child's parents know how you are preparing your child so they can review the same things with their child.

Regardless of what you do to get your child ready for it, the play date will go better with advance practice. Try to make sure he and his friend are familiar with the toys or games and have had a chance to play with them in different ways beforehand. For example, it will be easier for your child to take turns when the children play restaurant if he has practised being both the waiter and the customer with you first. Not only will he have words and ideas to bring to the play with his friend, he'll also know that it's fun to take on both roles.

Now that Gracie has practised being the customer and the waiter with her father, she's ready to take her friend's order.

Before the play date, it's also a good idea to listen to other young children talking together. That way you can learn their slang and practise the same words and phrases with your child. Remember that children often have two forms of social talk—one for adults and one for other children. The phrases that work for one group don't always work for the other. For example, "Hey" followed by a high-five might be the way your child's pals say hello. Or, instead of "good job," "cool" might be the compliment they use. You want your child to sound like other children, not like a mini-adult.

Discuss what a friend is

Sometimes talking about what a friend is can remind children how to act when they're with their friend. On the next page (under "What a Friend Is") are six suggestions for what to include when you discuss friendship with your child. Make your discussion personal and specific.

For example, if you're talking about one of the first two points, have your child name the interests that he shares or doesn't share with his friend. You can write the names of the toys and activities on a piece of paper and include a few pictures. (See next page, "What Ben and I Like," for an example of how your list might look.) If your child doesn't know his friend's likes and dislikes, have him think about some questions he can ask to find out.

What a Friend Is

- Friends like some of the same things.
- Friends like some different things.
- Friends stay and play together.
- Friends ask each other questions to find out what they like.
- Friends look at each other and listen to each other.
- Friends say nice things to each other.

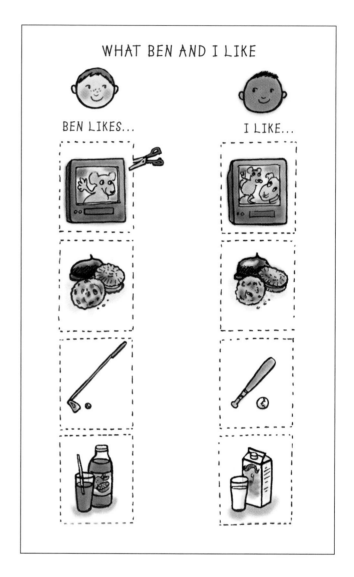

WHAT BEN AND I LIKE

BEN LIKES...   I LIKE...

Rehearse with your child alone

You can prepare your child for the play date in more detail by talking about specific things he can do and say when he gets together with his friend. Back up your discussion with some written reminders on a piece of paper or cue cards. You can prepare these visual helpers ahead of time or simply write and draw as you talk (stick figures will work). When you read Chapter 13, you'll find more ideas on how to use visual helpers to support your child's budding friendships.

Practising with Dad helps Trey remember to say the right thing when he's playing with his friend.

Too many suggestions will confuse your child. So pick one or two things he needs to be reminded of. For example, if your child needs to work on complimenting his friend, make a page with some examples of nice things he can say (like the one on the left).

Talk about ways to initiate play

Before the play date, familiarize your child with how he can greet his friend. Encourage a child who's new at socializing with other children to go to the door and say hi.

If your child needs to work on getting the play going, talk about ways he can do that. For example, tell him he can start play by joining in with what his friend is doing. Or he can take out a toy he knows his friend will like and ask his friend if he wants to play a game with it together. Use the ideas in the cue cards at the end of this chapter ("How to start playing with your friend") to guide your discussion. Remember to personalize your suggestions so they are specific. That means you should mention the playmate's name and the activities or toys. ("Liam likes to play basketball and so do you. You can ask him if he wants to play a game with you.")

Being sociable takes practice. Peter works on what to say before his friend arrives.

Talk about ways to continue the play

To decide what to practise, think of what skill is important for your child to remember: staying, playing, talking, tuning in and so on. For example, if your child is just starting to play near his friend, you might say ahead of time, "Stay with Evan and play dinosaurs together." If your goal is to have your child problem-solve or tune in to his friend's feelings, you might try a "What if" conversation, as Ben's father does in the picture below.

Practise "What if" situations before your child's play date so your child will be ready when things don't go as he expects.

Again, you can use the ideas at the end of this chapter ("How to keep on playing with your friend") to help your child keep the play going. It's up to you how to present them—verbally only or with cue cards.

Talk about ways to end the play

There are some tried-and-true endings that your child can memorize, such as "Let's do something else" or "I don't want to play this any more." Cue cards (see "How to finish playing with your friend" at the end of this chapter) can remind him how to exit gracefully instead of just getting up and walking away from his friend.

Discuss the play after your child's friend arrives

How much you tell your child's friend and his parent about your child's challenges is entirely up to you. Many young children accept people's differences without thinking twice about them. But at five years of age or so, children might start asking questions about why your child does certain things, such as "Why does he always wear baggy clothes?" or "Why does he cover his ears?" or "Why doesn't he answer me?"

If you get this kind of question, try answering simply and honestly. Focus on individual differences by saying something like, "He feels things more than you and me, so he wears clothes that don't touch him too much," or just say, "Tight clothes hurt his skin." To explain why he covers his ears, you might say, "He hears differently and some noises seem louder to him than they do to you or me. So he covers his ears to keep the sound out." Respond to "Why doesn't he answer me?" in a similar way, saying something like, "Some people find it hard to hear others when they're concentrating on something else. That's why he doesn't always answer you."

Teach your child's friend some coaching skills

Sometimes you might need to ask your child's playmate to do more than just play. For example, if your child is one who doesn't always respond, give his friend some tips about what to do beforehand ("Make sure you go right up to him so he sees you when you talk"). If initiating play is difficult for your child, you might coach his friend by saying something like, "When you want him to play, get close to him first and show him a toy that he likes. Then ask him to play with you."

Talk to the two children about the toys and activities

Your child's friend will need a few minutes' preparation so that his idea of how the play date will go is the same as your child's. So talk to the children together about what and how they can play. If the children seem to have a clear idea of what to do, you won't have to say much. Remember that the more the children can do themselves, the less coaching you'll have to do. But if it looks like the children need a helping hand, you might have to step in right at the beginning.

For example, if the children plan to play grocery store, you can ask them who they want to pretend to be ("Who wants to be the grocery man and who wants to be the shopper?"). If they don't come up with their own ideas about a possible script, make suggestions. If the children are going to play grocery store, you might say something like, "The shopper can ask, 'How much are the cookies, Mr. Grocery Man?'" Or if they're going to act out a birthday party, remind them about setting the table, giving presents and singing "Happy Birthday" to the birthday boy or girl.

If your child has a very hard time staying and playing with his friend, having a visual schedule with a picture of each activity might help both children do the same things at the same time. Include some choices in the schedule to encourage some early problem solving.

Seeing a schedule of what they're supposed to do can help keep children playing together.

You might also discuss how friends act. Look at the following picture to see how Jack's mother reminds Jack and his friend to use compliments when they play.

Let's think of some nice things we can say to each other before we play. If Jack throws the ball and it doesn't go in, what could you say, Ben?

Nice try.

Have the children role-play before the real play.

Helping your child make friends requires more than just inviting another child over and putting the toys out. A little extra time spent in planning will make the play date go better. In this chapter we talked about all the things that you can do to set up a play date: find the right friends, toys and activities and rehearse the play even before your child's friend arrives. Now read on to find out how your role as play coach changes once the children are playing together.

Parents can photocopy page 181 and cut out the cue cards they think will help their child interact with other children. Remember: show only one card at a time.
For all other uses, contact info@hanen.org for permission.

How to start playing with your friend

Be near your friend.

Tap your friend on his shoulder.

Smile and look at your friend.

Say "Hi" and use your friend's name.

Say something nice.

Ask your friend to play.

How to keep on playing with your friend

Stay with your friend.

Play with your friend.

Talk to your friend.

Parents can photocopy page 182 and cut out the cue cards they think will help their child interact with other children. Remember: show only one card at a time.
For all other uses, contact info@hanen.org for permission.

Ask for things you want.

Say something nice.

Answer your friend's questions.

Ask your friend a question.

Say something about what your friend says.

Talk about problems.

How to finish playing with your friend

Tell your friend.

Thank your friend.

Step Out… and Step In Again

12

After you've set up the play, your next job as play coach is to step out of the play and stand by. That means leaving your child and his friend alone to play until your help is needed. If you're too involved in the play, the children will talk to you and not to each other.

But at some point, you'll probably find that your child and his friend are stuck and need your guidance to keep their play going. In this chapter, you'll learn when and how to step in again, to lend a helping hand.

When to Step In

So long as your child and his friend are playing well together, leave them alone but stay nearby, ready to step in if necessary. You should be about three meters (10 feet) away and able to hear what they say.

If the children's play breaks down in some way, it's time to step in. Stepping in means that you help the children get back on track, either by coaching from where you are (outside the play) or else joining their play for a short time. Try your best to coach from outside the play. If that doesn't work, you'll have to coach from the inside by moving to where the children are and joining in their play.

Here are a few guidelines to help you decide when to step in and coach the children, either from the outside or the inside.

> **Step in and coach when:**
>
> > **The children aren't staying together**
> > **The children aren't playing together**
> > **The children aren't talking to each other** (even though they have some social play skills), or most of their talk seems directed at you
> > **The children get stuck** (in an argument or doing the same things over and over)—If the argument doesn't seem serious and no one is getting hurt, give the children a chance to work it out themselves.

During your child's first play dates, you'll probably have to step in and coach more often. Keep in mind, though, that your expectations should match your child's stage of social play.

For example, if your child is just beginning to play with other children, then you can expect the two of them to play side by side but not necessarily to talk to each other. To get your child to join in, you might simply make a suggestion about playing together and give him a toy that will make staying and playing more likely to happen.

Even when the children are talking to one another, remember that they don't need to talk the whole time that they play together. Expect them to say something to each other about five times during each play activity. Use your own common sense in deciding when to step in. But don't spoil the fun by stepping in too often.

Coach from Outside the Play

When you coach from the sidelines, give the children the least amount of help they need to succeed. Offer more help only as they need it. The I-Cues give you a framework for your coaching.

Interpret

Sometimes one child does or says something that the other child doesn't understand. For example, your child might stand next to his friend when he wants to play with him. You know what he wants to say but the other child doesn't. Or one child might say something that is hard to understand because he mispronounces some words, mixes up his sentences or speaks too softly for his friend to hear.

When these breakdowns in communication happen, be the child's interpreter. Put into words what you think he is trying to tell his playmate with his gestures and actions. Say what he's trying to say more clearly. Then wait for the children to pick up their conversation where they left off.

Mom interprets for Julian to help Andrew understand what Julian is telling him.

The Cues

The Cues discussed in earlier chapters will also help you be a better play coach. Use them to signal your ideas to one or both of the children until they're playing well again. As usual, keep your help to a minimum by using Cues that offer the least amount of help necessary.

> **Cues from the Coach's Corner**
>
> > Visual cues   **LEAST HELP**
> > Questions
> > Hints
> > Suggestions
> > Tell the child what to do or say   **MOST HELP**

Visual cues

If your child or his friend gets stuck and can't think of something to do or say, gently point to a prop or toy that might give him or her an idea of how to move on.

Mom helps Thomas figure out what to say by showing him a toy thermometer.

For a child who still needs help finding the words to say, cue cards can remind him what to say without your having to constantly tell him out loud. You could try showing your child a few cue cards with key phrases written on them, such as, "It's your turn" or "Let's play again." If you haven't made any cue cards ahead of time (like the ones on pages 181–182), just write down a few words or phrases as your child needs them.

Questions

Sometimes asking a question will help your child and his friend move forward in their play. For example, if the "doctor" doesn't seem to know what to do when the "mommy" brings the "baby" to him, you might say something like, "Mommy thinks her baby has a fever," and then ask, "What does the doctor do now?"

Hints

Remember that we've described a hint as "a general comment that gives your child an idea of what he could do or say next" (see page 64). You're asking one or both children to guess from your words what you think they could do.

For instance, if one child has all the crayons, you could say something to the other child like, "I think Matthew has some crayons for you." This is a hint for Matthew to offer his friend a crayon or for the other child to ask Matthew for one, without directly telling them to do either of those things.

Mom's hint gives Maya an idea of what to say when pretending to buy lemonade.

Suggestions

Chapter 4 explained that "suggestions are more specific than hints, but they still don't tell your child exactly what to do or say" (see page 65). Suggestions come in handy when one of the children talks to you instead of his friend.

For example, your child might want you to take on the role of a firefighter in his imaginary play. You could first try directing his attention back to his friend with a hint: "Maybe Ben wants to be the firefighter." If this kind of cue doesn't work, follow up with a suggestion, in which you tell him what to do but without giving him the exact script: "You could ask Ben if he wants to be the firefighter."

Mom suggests to Ali that he make Ben the other firefighter, instead of her.

It's okay to have a very short conversation with either child. But try to direct the child's interest back to his playmate as quickly as possible.

I need a leash.

Yes, so you can take your dog on a walk. You could ask Ben if he has a leash for sale.

Mom adds an idea about the leash. Then she directs the conversation away from herself by suggesting that Ali talk to Ben, who is pretending to be the cashier.

Tell the child what to do or say

Sometimes, a hint or a suggestion won't work. This usually happens when children are unfamiliar with an activity (such as a new pretend-play situation) and don't know what to do. When they need more direct help than a hint or a suggestion would provide, you can tell them exactly what to say. For example, if Ali isn't able to follow up on his mother's suggestion that he could ask Ben if he wants to be the firefighter, she could try saying to him, "Ali, ask Ben: 'Do you want to be a firefighter, too?'"

When arguments develop, children often forget all about words. Instead of talking through problems, some children, especially those who have trouble communicating, resort to pushing, grabbing or hitting. If that happens, you might find it better to give your child something to say right away.

Ask Emma for the doll. Say, "Can I please have a turn?"

To prevent a fight between the children, give your child the words to solve the problem.

Join in the Play

Sometimes coaching from the side is not enough. For example, when the children are involved in pretend play and are stuck doing the same thing over and over, you may need to step in and show them a new or different way to play. You should be familiar with how to get inside the play from reading Chapter 9.

Let's review how you can join in the play. First, get down to the children's level and play alongside them as if you were another child. Then follow the children's lead. That means if the children are pretending, take on a role (such as the monster, the little pig or the grocer). Act and sound like your make-believe character. Talk to the children as if they were characters in the make-believe ("Wake up, Superman! The world needs your help!").

Remember to play for a short time only and then step out again, so that the children can get back to playing with each other. If you look at the pictures below, you'll have an idea of how to step in, add something new and then step out.

Connor and Nigel are playing restaurant. Connor has been serving Nigel one pretend hot dog after the other. Nigel just keeps paying for his hot dog and ordering another one. Nigel's mother decides it's time for her to join the play and break the repeating pattern.

Here's your hot dog.

Nigel and Connor have been playing the same way for 20 minutes.

Do you have any food for my baby?

I have hot dogs!

To add a new idea to their pretend play, Nigel's mom steps in and pretends she's a customer looking for something for her baby to eat.

Nigel's mom suggests that he think of something the baby can eat at the restaurant, and he does.

Mom's getting ready to step out by directing Nigel's attention back to Connor.

Mom steps out, offers a new idea and lets the children continue playing together.

At the play date, you're going to be a coach to both children, stepping in when needed and stepping out when they play and talk together. Some parents will be tempted to step in more than they should. Others will want to stay on the sidelines when the children could really use some help.

As a general rule, the more the children can do without you, the better it is for their relationship. Even the best of friends, however, will disagree and argue. In the last chapter, we'll look at how to handle the inevitable meltdowns, tantrums or fights that happen when young children play together.

13

Use Visual Helpers to Show Your Child How to Be a Friend

No matter how well you plan your child's play dates, things can go wrong. Most young children find it hard to share toys, to wait for their turn and to play games that they haven't chosen. When things don't go their way, children often resort to tantrums, hitting, crying or pushing.

Working out frustrations will be easier for your child once he understands the other child's point of view. When he can consider how his actions affect his friend, he'll be able to think about different ways to act in those difficult moments.

In this chapter, you'll learn how to use a special set of visual helpers— including hand-drawn pictures, personalized stories and homemade videos— to coach your child through sticky social situations.

Tuning In to Solve Problems

There's always a reason for what any child does, and this simple rule applies to play dates as well. If you're tuned in to the children's feelings as they play, you'll have a better idea of what to do when one child starts hitting his playmate, crying or having a tantrum—or even repeating lines from videos over and over. Sometimes a strategy as basic as having two of the same toy (so that each child has his own to play with) may keep your child's play date on track.

But the tuning in that concerns us most in this chapter is the tuning in that should be happening between your child and his playmate. Most often play between children breaks down because one or both of them can't tune in to the other's thoughts and feelings. A child who is sensitive to his playmate's preferences and can accept his ideas makes a better friend. To succeed at friendship, your child needs to tune in to solve problems and, better still, to prevent them from occurring in the first place.

It's mine.

Think about the situation shown here. Jeremy is crying because his friend, Sam, has taken his toy car away from him. Sam has trouble sharing his favourite toy, so he finds the quickest and easiest way to get what he wants—grabbing it for himself—and Jeremy responds with tears. Neither child has considered how his actions might make his friend feel.

It's impossible for your child to make and keep friends just by following specific guidelines about what to say, where to stand or how loudly to talk. Knowing some of the rules of social etiquette is a good start, but he also needs an understanding of how his actions affect his friend's feelings.

Problem-solving skills

Children who are tuned in to other children have a set of problem-solving skills to draw on when they play with their friends. If Sam had thought about how his unwillingness to share would make his friend feel, he might have behaved differently. He also might have chosen a different way to get the car if he had realized that his friend loved that toy so much.

Use the checklist on the next page to find the skills that your child has and the ones he's missing. As you read this chapter, you can use this information to decide which skills he'll need your help to learn.

Talk problems through

There is nothing wrong with discussing friendship issues without visual helpers. In fact, many verbal children, especially those with Asperger syndrome, often prefer this way of working things out. In any case, sometimes you won't have a pencil and paper handy or there won't be time to draw or write.

Problem-Solving Skills Checklist

	NEVER	SOMETIMES	OFTEN
1. Uses problem-solving words	◯	◯	◯
2. Understands how others might think or feel	◯	◯	◯
3. Understands consequences of his actions	◯	◯	◯
4. Compromises (for example, is willing to play games his friend suggests)	◯	◯	◯
5. Accepts mistakes of others	◯	◯	◯
6. Copes with change	◯	◯	◯
7. Knows when someone is being unfriendly	◯	◯	◯

That's when it's probably faster and easier to talk about what's happening and, together with your child and his friend, come up with a possible solution to the problem. For example, during the fight over the car between Jeremy and Sam, Sam's mother might have stepped in right away and suggested that Sam find another car for his friend Jeremy to play with.

In Chapter 9 you learned some ways to talk through problems with your child. Those same tips for solving problems that you encounter as you play with your child should now come in handy when your child and his friend run into difficulties. Let's review them here (see pages 150–151 for details):

> Plan ahead to avoid problems later.
> Use problem-solving words (for example, "now/later," "is/isn't a good idea," "some/all," "same/different" and "either/or").
> Focus on the positive.
> Talk about how people are feeling.
> Talk about consequences of what the child is doing.
> Teach the child something different to say or do to replace socially unacceptable behaviour.
> Help the child figure out what else he can do.
> Use a visual helper to work out the problem.
> Choose your battles. (Ignore mild disagreements between the children.)

Visual Helpers to Teach Friendship Skills

There are advantages to using a hand-written story or a drawing when you discuss difficult moments with your child. Some children actually learn better by looking at printed words, pictures or videos. In addition, unlike spoken words, printed words and drawings last a long time. With visual helpers, your child has a written record of his actions, which he can reread and keep on learning from.

There are many different ways to use visual helpers to teach your child about the ins and outs of social situations, but here we're going to focus on three:

> Social Stories
> Comic Strip Conversations
> Video modelling

While you might find it easier to work with a professional (such as a teacher or a speech language pathologist) who is familiar with writing Social Stories and Comic Strip Conversations, many parents have great success creating their own for their children. You can even write the stories *with* your child. There are specific guidelines for the stories, but don't be afraid of adapting them to your needs.

Social Stories

Developed by Carol Gray, Social Stories™ are a way to give your child information about a specific social situation using your own personalized stories. Normally quite short—just two to twelve sentences long—these stories describe how people act and feel in difficult situations and give your child some ideas about what he could do or say in those situations. While the stories are helpful in improving your child's behaviour, they can also just be a celebration of all the things he's doing right.

You can read one of Carol Gray's books for detailed guidelines for writing the stories. Here is a short summary to get you started:

> Identify a friendship skill that you want to celebrate or one your child needs help with (such as winning or losing games, sharing or taking turns).
> Think of a title that asks a question that the story will answer or describes what the story will be about ("What My Friends Like").
> Write from your child's point of view. ("My name is Sam. Sometimes my friend Jeremy comes to play at my house.")
> Tell what's happening (what, where, when, who, how and why). Most of your story will be made up of descriptive sentences about how some other people felt in a similar situation and how they acted positively ("William lets me play with his trains when I'm at his house"). Write your descriptive sentences in the third person ("He asks...," "Penny plays..."). Use the word "sometimes" so your child will understand that the situation might change under different circumstances. ("Sometimes, when my friends are playing a game, I want to play a different one.")
> Use positive sentences in your story. (Instead of, "Peter doesn't look away when he talks to me," say something like, "Peter looks at me when he talks to me.")
> At the end of your story, you could (but don't have to) suggest a new strategy for your child to try in the difficult social situation and describe how others will react to him if he acts in a positive way—for example, "When people talk to me, I will try to look at them. Then they will know that I'm listening to them." Another example: "I will try to let Jeremy play

with my car when he's at my house. Then Jeremy will be happy, Mom will be happy and Jeremy will want to play with me again." You don't want your child to think he has to use the suggestion all of the time, so it's important that you use some words to show possibilities, such as "try" and "might."

> Add some pictures to illustrate your story, if you're comfortable making simple drawings and if you think they will help your child understand and remember the story.

The following Social Story might help Sam share his car with Jeremy next time they play together. Notice how most of the sentences describe the situation. There are no negative descriptions such as, "I don't like Jeremy to play with my car," and there is only one suggestion of what Sam might do.

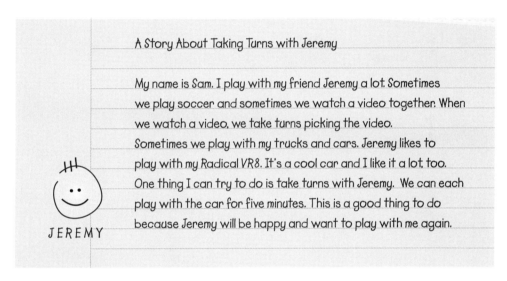

A Story About Taking Turns with Jeremy

My name is Sam. I play with my friend Jeremy a lot. Sometimes we play soccer and sometimes we watch a video together. When we watch a video, we take turns picking the video.
Sometimes we play with my trucks and cars. Jeremy likes to play with my Radical VR8. It's a cool car and I like it a lot, too.
One thing I can try to do is take turns with Jeremy. We can each play with the car for five minutes. This is a good thing to do because Jeremy will be happy and want to play with me again.

JEREMY

Here's another example of a story, written for Michael, who gets upset when other children try to help him. Notice how it's written to be interactive—Mom leaves the list of ways children have been helpful blank, so that Michael can complete it himself.

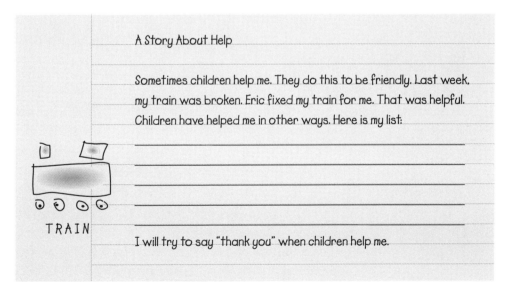

A Story About Help

Sometimes children help me. They do this to be friendly. Last week, my train was broken. Eric fixed my train for me. That was helpful.
Children have helped me in other ways. Here is my list:

_____

_____

_____

_____

_____

TRAIN

I will try to say "thank you" when children help me.

You can write a Social Story about things your child could say to make his conversations with his friends go better. The following story talks about giving compliments to people. Notice again that there's just one suggestion given at the end of the story.

That smells good!

> ### A Story About Compliments
>
> People like to get compliments. Compliments are nice things to say to people when they try to do a good job. Compliments make people feel happy. When Mom or Dad want to make people feel happy, they give compliments. When Mom cooks dinner, Dad sometimes says "That smells good."
> Children give compliments, too. When I made a tower, Ben said, "Cool!" Here are some other compliments: "I like that!" "High-five!" "Good job!"
> I will try to give compliments when someone tries to do a good job.

One of the best ways to be friendly is to ask questions about your friend's interests. Initiating conversation in this way is hard for Simon, so his mother writes him the following story. Notice how the story uses a fill-in-the-blanks format so Simon can reach his own conclusions.

> ### What I Can Ask Spencer About
>
> I often talk about trains. I often think about _____ .
> I often talk about computer games. I often think about ___ _____.
> Spencer often talks about dinosaurs. I guess Spencer thinks about
> _____ .
> Spencer may like it if I ask him about_____ .

Make the reading interactive

Reading a Social Story shouldn't be a passive experience for your child. If he can read it himself, let him. If you're doing the reading, remember the Four S's. Say Less —if you find the sentences you wrote are too long, simplify as you read them. And just as with books, your child has to be interested in what you're reading to get something out of the experience, so remember to Stress —make important words stand out.

If you've added pictures to your story, show them to your child and encourage him to talk about them. For example, when Sam's mom reads to her son "A Story About Taking Turns with Jeremy," she can stop before the end, point to the picture of the smiling face and ask why Jeremy is smiling ("Jeremy's happy because he has a turn to play with the car"). Then, before reading the end of the story, Mom can ask Sam to think about the consequences of his positive behaviour ("Jeremy will want to play with Sam again").

While reading the story, your child might think of something else to tell you. As long as it's related to what you're talking about, take the time to include his interests and then get back to the story.

Comic Strip Conversations

Comic Strip Conversations, also developed by Carol Gray, show children how conversations work using simple cartoon-style drawings that you create as you talk. The words you write in the talk bubbles and thought bubbles will give your child ideas about what to say. They'll also let him know what the people around him are thinking and feeling.

You can use Comic Strip Conversations at the moment your child's play date runs into trouble. Or you can use them afterward, to review with your child what has happened. You can even use them before the play date, to prepare your child for dealing with problems that might crop up. Jeremy's mom has stepped in to her son's play date to draw the following examples "on the spot."

The minute she sees Sam ignoring Jeremy, Sam's mom draws a picture to show Sam what his friend is thinking.

Then, Mom gives Sam an idea in writing about something he could say, as well as a plan for him to think about.

Here's how Sam's mother could use a similar Comic Strip Conversation after his play date with Jeremy has ended. Through pictures and printed words, she could help Sam see how his actions made his friend feel and what other choices he could make in the future.

Mom shows Sam what happened, and talks about how Jeremy felt.

After reviewing what happened at the play date, Mom could then continue the Comic Strip Conversation to help Sam see some other ways of solving the problem next time around.

Video modelling

Many children are enthusiastic video watchers. This isn't necessarily a bad thing; they can learn a lot of language and actions from movies and television shows.

You can take advantage of this natural interest by making home movies of your child playing with another child at his play date. Videos of this kind provide many opportunities for the two of you to talk about why people do certain things and how they feel. Seeing himself in action will help your child think about what he could do next time. In general, it's best to emphasize the positive. By showing him what he looks like and sounds like when he's playing successfully with his friend, you'll reinforce his good behaviour.

Begin by identifying the friendship skills you want to highlight. For instance, you could concentrate on sharing toys with a friend, accepting help, giving compliments or asking a friend questions about his interests.

Filming and editing

After you've decided what skill you want to highlight, videotape your child playing with his friend in a situation in which he'll need to use that skill. You might have to videotape several different times over a period of a few days to have enough positive examples—about two and a half minutes' worth—to show your child.

The idea is for your child to see himself at his best, especially if he's trying to improve on something he's already doing. To make sure you get the video you want, you can also try telling your child exactly what to say. When you edit your film later on, you can edit your words out. (Note that being directive in this way is only recommended to get an ideal video, and not for everyday interactions!)

Dad captures just the right moment in this video. When Sam watches the movie later, he'll see that sharing toys with Jeremy makes his friend happy.

It's possible, too, to make a video with children other than your child demonstrating the friendship skill you're focusing on. At the time this book is being written, there is no research showing that your child does better watching himself than he would watching other children. For learning brand new skills, a video of other children might do the trick.

In the situation shown in the picture on the next page, Riley's mom thinks Riley could have better play dates if he learned how to ask his friend some questions about himself. Riley's mother can't get a video of Riley asking these kinds of questions, so instead she videotapes Riley's father and his sister, Briana, asking and answering one another's questions.

After videotaping the play date, edit out all but the most positive examples of the skill that you want to focus on. There is software that lets you edit tapes from a digital camcorder to a computer. If, however, you don't have a way to edit, just fast-forward over the negative parts. It's important that your child see himself doing the right thing.

You could ask me about my day.

What did you do today, Mom?

After watching the video in which Riley's sister and father ask each other some personal questions, Mom suggests that Riley ask her a question just as he saw his sister, Briana, do in the video.

Watching and trying it out

Before sharing the video with your child, introduce it by talking a little bit about what your child is going to see. You can give the video a title, just as you do when you write a Social Story. For example, Sam's mother might say, "Let's watch the video of you taking turns with Jeremy."

At the end of the video (if he's still paying attention), describe the reaction of the other child to your child, just as you might do in a Social Story. Sam's mom might end his video by saying something like, "When you gave Jeremy your car, he looked happy. He probably will want to play with you again."

Try to watch the tape a couple of times during the week. Always watch for one thing only at a time, even if the video has examples of other things you want your child to see. You can watch the same video for another reason at a different time.

Once your child has watched the video you've made for him, set up a similar situation in real life where he can try out the very friendship skill he's watched on video.

Other ways to use video

The possibilities for using video are endless. You've already read in Chapter 2, for example, about pausing videos at key moments so your child can identify the emotion on someone's face and think about why that person is feeling that way. Video lets your child focus on aspects of communication that he might forget about in the excitement of the moment—things like how loudly people are talking and how their tone of voice reveals their feelings. And just by watching with the volume off, your child has a chance to think about all the ways people communicate without words (the looks on their faces and what they do with their hands).

Many children have trouble knowing where to stand when they talk to others. Your child might talk to people when he's on the other side of the room. Or he might do the opposite, getting too close to the person he's talking to. If that's the case, pause the video every so often and comment on where the person in the video is standing. ("Look at how close he's standing, and how he's looking right at his friend's face. That's how best friends talk to each other.") This is a good skill to try out in real life after watching the video.

Tips on Where to Stand

You can use video to show your child where people stand when they talk to each other. It may help your child remember what to do if you teach him some names for the spaces: "family," "friendly" and "far-away."

The Family Space
Family members and best friends stand very close to each other when they talk, no more than at arms length and sometimes almost touching.

The Friendly Space
Other friends stand a bit farther apart when they're talking—about four feet away.

The Far-Away Space
There is an area beyond four feet where limited conversation takes place. When you notice a person you know at this distance, you can begin a conversation by calling out his name and shouting hello. Then one of you might move into the family space or the friendly space if you want to continue the conversation.

If you're a techno wizard, you can make a video to illustrate a Social Story. For example, a video about the story "What I Can Ask People About" might show a few people talking about their favourite subject and a few others asking them questions about it.

If you don't have the technical skills or enough time to make your own films, you can watch children's videos or appropriate adult shows in the same way. Just remember to focus on the positive, even when it's not your child up on the screen.

· ·

For visual learners, getting information through hand-written or hand-drawn stories or homemade movies can be a lot of fun. By seeing himself in successful social situations—initiating conversation, considering other people's feelings or replacing negative behaviours with positive ones—your child will have his best self as a model.

The Last Word

This book has presented many strategies for helping your child develop better people skills. If you've been trying out the ideas as you read, his "talkability" has probably already improved. That means he's now trying to understand more than just what people say and to use his talking for true back-and-forth conversations.

There's no way any parent can prepare a child for all of life's ups and downs. Sometimes your child might fit in with his peer group, and at other times he might not. At those times, when he feels left out or different, he'll rely on something else he's learned from you—he'll cope best if he feels good about himself. By talking and playing with your child in a positive way, you'll help your child realize that he is valued and loved by the most important people in his life.